The
EXODUS
Experience

SHIN: *The letter* shin *stands for God's name* El Shaddai, *the mountain God and God the All-powerful One, who liberates the Israelites and each person from the bondage of slavery and brings them into the Promised Land.*

When you look at the form of shin, *you can see the burning bush silhouetted against the horizon. You can also see a tree with branches, a vase of flowers, a frail piece of bark on the sea of life, and a candle holder spreading light to a darkened world.*

This letter is so important that it is embossed on the doorpost of Jewish homes, and it is kissed upon entering and leaving the house. It is a reminder of God's presence everywhere.

The
EXODUS
Experience

A JOURNEY IN PRAYER

by
Maureena Fritz, NDS

SAINT MARY'S PRESS
CHRISTIAN BROTHERS PUBLICATIONS
WINONA, MINNESOTA

To my parents,
Maura and Simon Fritz,
and to the Sisters of Sion at 333 Acadia Drive

Acknowledgments

I am deeply grateful to the Sisters of Sion at Acadia, Saskatoon, particularly to Sr. Marian Dolan, who proofread the first draft of the manuscript, and to the Sisters of Saint Joseph at Saint Joseph Hospital, Brantford, Ontario, for their hospitality during the preparation of the manuscript.

Thanks also to Gloria Ridler, who typed the original manuscript. I am indebted to Anne Anderson, CSJ, for manuscript refinements and to M. Josephine Flaherty, PhD, who spent many hours proofreading the final draft of the manuscript.

The acknowledgments continue on page 151.

The publishing team for this book included Robert P. Stamschror, development editor; Susan Baranczyk, manuscript editor; Hollace Storkel, typesetter; and Evy Abrahamson, cover artist.

Printed in the United States of America

Printing: 6 5 4 3 2

Year: 1995 94 93 92 91 90 89

ISBN 0-88489-186-0

Contents

Preparing the Way

The Scriptures are the word of God.

The Scriptures are the word about God. They reveal to us who God is: "'a God merciful and gracious, slow to anger, and abounding in steadfast love and faithfulness'" (Exod. 34:6). The Scriptures are the revelation of a God who creates, redeems, and glorifies.

The Scriptures are also the word about human persons and human community in every place and every age—humans who possess inclinations toward good and inclinations toward evil. They reveal the human destiny—to become free and glorious daughters and sons of God. They reveal the way to this freedom and fulfillment.

The Scriptures are not only the word about God and humans but also the word that communicates between God and humans. They are the word that discloses and opens the Divine and human persons to one another and that brings about union.

Consequently, when we read the scriptural story of God and the Israelites in the Book of Exodus, it becomes our story. The Israelites' encounter with God becomes our encounter with God. Our experience is a microcosm of that experience. We know liberation from oppressive regimes. We have our deserts and our Sinais. We meet the Pharaoh and the Moses figures in the world—those who destroy life and those who give life. We find within each one of us a Moses and a Pharaoh, an Aaron and a Miriam, an Egypt, a desert, a Sinai, and a Promised Land. And present in all of these occurrences is a God, freeing us and saving us.

The findings of modern human sciences support the use of the historical drama of Exodus as an allegory of our spiritual journey. Sigmund Freud told us of the multidimensional character of the human personality with its id, ego, and superego. He found that each of us has a personal unconscious—with feelings, memories, and images—that constantly interacts with and influences the conscious level of our life.

Carl Jung, probing even deeper, concluded that the human person possesses not only a *personal* unconscious (out of which yearnings, ideas, and actions are prompted) but also a *collective* unconscious, which contains the memories and patterns of the behavior of our ancestors.

Other psychologists, psychotherapists, and dream analysts, following Freud and Jung, have discovered further dimensions of the human person that contain years and years of ancestral human experience, thoughts, feelings, and motivations—both evil and good, demonic and divine.

Psychologists are not alone in giving an account of the human mystery. Literary and spiritual writers do so as well. In the modern novel *Steppenwolf,* we read of a man who is both man and wolf, sinner and saint, body and spirit:

> For there is not a single human being . . . who is so conveniently simple that [their] being can be explained as the sum of two or three principal elements; and to explain so complex a man as Harry by the artless division into wolf and man is a hopelessly childish attempt. Harry consists of a hundred or a thousand selves, not of two. His life oscillates, as everyone's does, not merely between two poles, such as the body and the spirit, the saint and the sinner, but between thousands. . . . (Hermann Hesse, pp. 57–58)

Saint Teresa of Ávila, through the insight of contemplative prayer, saw worlds within worlds enveloped inside the human person. She compared the inner world of a person to an "interior castle"—a castle with moats and walls, reptiles and dragons, saintly characters and demonic characters. She saw palaces within palaces, seven of them, and on the throne of the seventh and most interior one, the Sovereign Creator of the world, enticing the soul to divine intimacy.

These nonscriptural accounts of the dimension of mystery in us make the Exodus story all the more credible as an allegorical account of the human experience infused with the Divine. Exodus gives us a particularly meaningful and hopeful way of understanding our human experience at a deeper level and a unique language by which to describe that experience. When we enter into this biblical drama, we live again our own drama, with its sufferings and comforts, fears and hopes, exiles and homecomings, wars and peacemakings. But in this reliving of the Scriptures, we have God present to us, with the promise and power that saved and freed the Israelites.

We can read the Book of Exodus, then, on two levels:

1. as an account of an actual historical people called out of a land of slavery into the Promised Land
2. as an allegorical description of our own exodus

We can come to understand that the journey from the land of slavery into the Promised Land is each one's journey from alienation from self and God to the promised land of integration and oneness with self, others, and God. We can meet the biblical characters in our own history and face within ourselves Pharaoh the tyrant, Moses the leader, Aaron the priest, and Miriam the prophet. We can pass through and over the Egypts, the Red Seas, the deserts, and the mountains in our own life, allowing God to test us, purify us, and lead us to divine intimacy.

Two important metaphors flow through the Book of Exodus: journey and temple.

Journey: The notion of a journey is a more apt image for the spiritual life than a stage theory that sees growth as steady development upward. A journey can have its ups and downs; it can be "there and back again." It is in the ups and downs and in the back and forth that spiritual deepening often takes place.

Temple: The image of a temple points to what we are to become. We are to become the living temple of the most-high God, as in the words of the Scriptures: "'. . . Let them make me a sanctuary, that I may dwell in their midst'" (Exod. 25:8).

Keeping in mind that the word of God in the Scriptures is not only a revelation of what happened long ago, "once upon a time," but also an allegorical description of what is happening now in our life, consider the following directions for the use of this prayer book.

Directions for the Use of This Book

The scriptural story of the Exodus journey can be insightful and inspiring for your own spiritual journey if you read and reflect on it with faith. This book of meditations is designed to help this kind of faith-filled reflection and can be used in several different situations:

- for daily prayer
- for extensive periods of prayer, such as during a retreat
- during a season of the liturgical year, such as Lent
- on the occasion of a particular event or circumstance, such as the death of a loved one or an important decision

The first time you use this book, follow the meditations in the sequence given. After discovering all the themes that the meditations contain, you might want to select meditations in a sequence that better fits your spiritual needs.

Some meditations can be completed in one prayer time or sitting. Other meditations will reach more deeply and more extensively into your life journey, so you might want to continue a meditation for several sittings. The standard steps of each meditation are given below, but before previewing them, consider the following recommendation:

If you are not acquainted with the Book of Exodus, read through the book, particularly the first twenty chapters. A reading of these chapters will make you familiar with the story and give you a sense of the flow of the meditations based on it.

The scriptural excerpts and references in this book are from the Revised Standard Version (RSV). In some places the translation has been adapted for the use of inclusive language.

The Steps of Each Meditation

Each meditation will follow a standard set of steps. You might find that this format will continue to serve you well. If, having followed these steps several times, you find that other rhythms and ways of entering into meditation work better, use them. However, it is recommended that in the beginning you follow these steps rather closely.

Hebrew letter: A letter of the Hebrew alphabet heads and serves as a motif for each part of this book and each meditation. The letters and their meanings will enrich your meditations and provide additional signposts of the progress of your spiritual journey. The Hebrew language is read from right to left. It will be important to remember this in order to receive the full impact of each letter's shape and meaning.

Introductory comments: The purpose of the introductory comments is to focus your reflections and to help you enter into the biblical text both as a historical account and as an allegory of your own life. If you meditate and pray in the direction set by the introduction, the journey will progress, and you will be introduced to the great themes of the spiritual journey as they occur in the Exodus story and in your own spiritual journey.

A passage from the Book of Exodus: Approximately ten to fifteen verses from the Book of Exodus are excerpted at the beginning of each meditation so that you have these verses immediately before you. Read that scriptural passage slowly and reflectively. You might want to read it more than once. Reading the Scriptures is like walking into a forest where you have never been before. When you first enter, you see no path. The more you walk the same route, the more visible the path becomes. The third or fourth time that you read the scriptural passage, let it speak directly to your own spiritual life.

Commentary: The commentary is a reflection on certain words and phrases of the biblical passage. The theme of the meditation is developed as these words and phrases connect and converge. You might experience this convergence as bewildering at first, but follow through with it. When the words and meanings in the commentary have had time to collect, you will see how they come together into the theme of the meditation.

Certain aspects of the commentary will touch you more than others do. Because it is not necessary to draw out all the meaning of the text at one time, feel free to spend more time with some aspects than with others.

Reflection and journal-writing exercises: The purpose of the reflection and journal-writing exercises is to help you make the transition from the biblical story to the experience of your own spiritual life.

Journal writing will be an important part of coming into contact with your own exodus. There is a difference between "keeping a journal" and "journal writing." Keeping a journal can mean a simple recording of events. Journal writing means that when you begin to write, you do not know what the result will be. You simply let your pen flow with your thoughts and feelings. As you write, new expressions, images, and feelings will appear. The expressions, images, and feelings themselves will be the guideposts to help you continue your journey and your journal writing.

Remember that there are no rights and wrongs in journal writing and that you need not worry about correct grammar or sentence structure. Your journal is meant for you alone. You need freedom and privacy in order to probe your thoughts and feelings, including those you have not dared to look at before.

In addition to helping you travel where you have not traveled before, journal writing provides a log of your journey. As you return again and again to meditate on the Israelites' Exodus, this record will allow you to see the distance that you have traveled and the graced events that took place at the time of writing. You will be able to compare that history with what is happening currently in your life. For easy reference, date your entries so you will know when you wrote them.

You need not wait until you reach the exercise step of the meditation to begin journal writing. Indeed, you are encouraged to do journal writing during each of the steps. At times you might write only a line or two, but if you use more than one prayer time for a meditation, these lines will help you pick up quickly from where you left off the time before.

If several reflection and journal-writing exercises are offered for a given meditation, do not feel obliged to do them all the first time that you do the meditation. Pick one or more that seem to fit best at the time. The others can be used if you choose to use the meditation again.

Memory verse: Each meditation closes with a verse from Psalm 119. The verses chosen from this psalm begin with the same Hebrew letter that introduces the meditation.

This closure has been chosen for both a biblical reason and a personal reason. The biblical reason is that through recitation of the Psalms, we become worthy to return to God. The personal reason flows from the biblical reason. Reciting a verse of the Psalms from time to time serves as a handle to keep us turned toward God throughout the day.

The verse chosen for each of the meditations is connected to the theme of the meditation. Each time you end a meditation, take this verse with you in your heart and on your lips.

You are now ready to begin your exodus. Although the way may not always be clear and may sometimes be fearful, it will be an exciting journey—one filled with promise and hope. Let the Lord's words to Jeremiah travel with you:

"Be not afraid . . .
for I am with you to deliver you. . . ."

(Jer. 1:8)

HEH: *The letter* heh *stands for God's most-special name, which is revealed to Moses in Exod. 3:14. This unique name has been variously translated as* Jehovah *and* Yahweh. *Out of respect for this most-holy name, many translators of the Bible write it* LORD, *in uppercase letters.*

In Bondage

An eagle that wanted to fly away from its home in the tall pine tree to the mountain across the valley was unable to take off. Its leg was tied by a fine string to one of the branches. Similarly, our sins and enslaving habits act as strings that prevent us from beginning the journey to the mountain of God.

The purposes of the meditations in part A are, first, to help you name and come in touch with what binds and enslaves you and, second, to lead you along a route with Moses, where you will be given a foretaste of the sweetness of divine intimacy promised to those who trust God.

Meditation 1 is a reflection on the names of the people in the Exodus story and what those people represent in yourself.

You will be encouraged to name and reflect on aspects of your life that enslave you and those that liberate you.

In meditation 2, the birth of Moses calls attention to the birthing process in your own life. Freedom from bondage and awakening to new life are related. Necessary conditions for new life will be considered.

In meditation 3, Moses, a prince in the court of Pharaoh, is forced to flee to the desert. There, alone and far from the corrupting influence of a cruel despot, he grows to manhood. Matured and purified in mind and heart, Moses is made ready for an encounter with God.

Meditation 4 describes Moses' encounter with God at the burning bush. Then, because encounters with God are never for oneself alone, meditation 5 describes the scene in which God commissions Moses to return and liberate the Israelites from Egypt. Moses' self-doubts assert themselves at the thought of returning to the place from which he has fled, yet he returns as a man who is different from the person he was when he left.

Meditation 6 relates the presence of divine assistance that accompanies one who responds to God's call—how in the face of uncertainties and dangers, God's promise, "I will be with you," is fulfilled.

As you meditate and relive your journey, you too will find that you are a different person than when you began. At least partially, the words of Isaiah's prophecy will be fulfilled in you after you have sojourned, like the Hebrews, in Egypt:

> You shall no more be termed Forsaken,
>   and your land shall no more be termed Desolate;
> but you shall be called My delight is in her,
>   and your land Married;
> for the LORD delights in you,
>
> .   .   .   .
>
> and as the bridegroom rejoices over the bride,
>   so shall your God rejoice over you.
>
>   (Isa. 62:4–5)

TSADI: Tsadi *stands for* tsedek, *which means* "righteousness." *The letter* tsadi *is like a person with head and foot bent forward in one direction and a hand in the other direction to provide balance. It also represents the scriptural righteous ones who, with their body and head bent toward God, are able to resist the evil forces in the world.*

Naming
My Slavery

On a journey, we like to know who our traveling companions are. The Book of Exodus begins with the phrase "These are the names." Naming was significant for the Israelites. The one who names demonstrates a knowledge of, a power over, and a responsibility for those named. Also, names indicate the character and destiny of those named. The names of the Twelve Tribes of Israel are given—names that stand for basic types of human persons: Reuben, who sees; Simeon, who hears; Levi, who is completely dedicated to God's service; Dan, who judges; and so on. A number of women are also part of the story: for example, Leah, who feels the least preferred of Jacob's two wives, and Shiphrah, who shines with indomitable courage. Of course, the name *Pharaoh* plays an important part in the Exodus story.

In recognizing these names and becoming acquainted with these characters, we can come to better know who we are because as we journey through life, we journey with a part of us who is Levi and a part who is Pharaoh.

Exodus 1:1–17

These are the names of the sons of Israel who came to Egypt
with Jacob, each with his household: Reuben, Simeon, Levi,
and Judah, Issachar, Zebulun, and Benjamin, Dan and
Naphtali, Gad and Asher. All the offspring of Jacob were
seventy persons; Joseph was already in Egypt. Then Joseph
died, and all his brothers, and all that generation. But the
descendants of Israel were fruitful and increased greatly;
they multiplied and grew exceedingly strong; so that the
land was filled with them.

Now there arose a new king over Egypt, who did not
know Joseph. And he said to his people, "Behold, the people of Israel are too many and too mighty for us. Come, let
us deal shrewdly with them, lest they multiply, and, if war
befall us, they join our enemies and fight against us and escape from the land." Therefore they set taskmasters over
them to afflict them with heavy burdens; and they built for
Pharaoh store-cities, Pithom and Raamses. But the more
they were oppressed, the more they multiplied and the
more they spread abroad. And the Egyptians were in dread
of the people of Israel. So they made the people of Israel
serve with rigor, and made their lives bitter with hard
service, in mortar and brick, and in all kinds of work in the
field; in all their work they made them serve with rigor.

Then the king of Egypt said to the Hebrew midwives,
one of whom was named Shiphrah and the other Puah,
"When you serve as midwife to the Hebrew women, and
see them upon the birthstool, if it is a son, you shall kill
him; but if it is a daughter, she shall live." But the midwives
feared God, and did not do as the king of Egypt commanded them, but let the male children live.

Commentary

Biblical names are important. They contain predictions of a
hoped-for future and are said to be clues to the nature of biblical characters. Israelite tradition holds that the name of a person influences the person's career.

In ancient Israel, according to custom, mothers named the children. Jacob was the father of the Twelve Tribes of Israel, but his two wives, Leah and Rachel, named the twelve sons. Each name was carefully chosen to indicate hopes for and important traits of the child.

Leah named these sons:
- *Reuben:* "to see"; he is preeminent in pride and power, and unstable as water.
- *Simeon:* "heard"; he grows to be a violent man, cursed by Jacob for his anger and cruelty.
- *Levi:* "to enjoin, accompany, escort"; he too is violent, but his descendants are redeemed and become the priestly tribe.
- *Judah:* "thanksgiving"; from him all the Jewish people receive their name, for the word *Jew* comes from *Judah*; Jesus is a descendant of this tribe.
- *Issachar:* "reward"; his name also means "strong ass" or "slave of forced labor."
- *Zebulun:* "honor"; he is a "haven for ships."
- *Gad:* "fortune"; his tribe is known for being warriors.
- *Asher:* "happy"; his tribe grows famous olive trees symbolic of joy and riches, and he is known for his wisdom.

Rachel named these sons:
- *Benjamin:* "son of the right hand"; he is called "a ravenous wolf."
- *Dan:* "judge"; Jacob blesses Dan, who "shall judge his people."
- *Naphtali:* "wrestler"; Jacob says that he is "'a hind let loose, that bears comely fawns'" (Gen. 49:21).
- *Joseph:* "to add"; the favorite son of Jacob, he is a "fruitful bough" and a "prince."

The time that the Twelve Tribes of Israel spend in Egypt marks a significant part of the Exodus journey and has special significance for the spiritual journey. From the Hebrew word for Egypt, *Mitzraim*, we receive a clue to the meaning of the Israelite sojourn there. *Mitzraim* means "limitation," "bondage," or "affliction." Egypt is the place where the Israelites became enslaved. Before these people experience freedom, they experience slavery.

At one time or another, *Mitzraim* reflects the condition of every person. Although we can be happy and fruitful, we can also be enslaved. Saint Paul wrote, "For I delight in the law of God, in my inmost self, but I see in my members another law at war with the law of my mind and making me captive to the law of sin which dwells in my members" (Rom. 7:22–23).

The new Pharaoh, not knowing Joseph or the people, fears the Twelve Tribes of Israel because, as he says, "'. . . If war befall us, they join our enemies and fight against us and escape from the land.'" If the Israelites escape, Egypt will lose its slave labor forces. Sometimes our positive characteristics are enslaved and held in bondage by forces within us too.

So Pharaoh shrewdly orders the midwives to put to death the Israelite male children while they are still upon the birth-stool, when even the mothers do not know what is happening. He also commands his people to cast into the river every Is-raelite male child who escapes death at birth. He does not give these orders to his chief executioners but rather tells the Egyptian people to carry them out. In this manner he escapes direct blame and allows innocent people to become victims of the lawless. Conditions worsen to the point that Israelite children are no longer safe in their own homes.

Great suffering often brings forth strong, compassionate people from both the oppressed and the oppressor. We see this in the story of the midwives, Shiphrah and Puah. *Shiphrah* means "brightness," and *Puah* means "splendid." These two women, who many scholars believe are Egyptian, each live up to their name. Fearing God, they refuse to obey Pharaoh's orders. Through their civil disobedience, a people survive extinction. The names of the twelve tribes live on, and the people of Israel begin the Exodus. We can begin our own exodus by identifying our "names"—the people inside us from whom we must escape and with whom we must journey.

Reflection and Journal-writing Exercises

1. You have met many characters in this chapter of Exodus, all of whom can represent some aspect of your spiritual experience or interior spiritual life. Getting to know all of these aspects of or characters in your spiritual life might take a lifetime, but you can begin to explore some of them now.
- From the list of biblical names on page 19, choose several whose characters seem to have a place in yourself.
- Choose one name that points to a bright side of yourself and one that points to a dark side.

2. Recognizing both the graced and the sinful sides of the self is important. To acknowledge that a cruel and ruthless Pharaoh resides within you might be difficult. At the same time, it might be difficult to recognize the good within yourself—for instance, a Levi (one totally committed to God), a Zebulun (a person of honor), or a Joseph (the favorite of his father).

In this exercise, focus on the dark and sinful side of your self.
- Pick one name from the list on page 19 that represents an aspect of yourself that keeps you in bondage.
- Imagine that aspect of yourself as a separate person.
- In your journal, write a letter to this person. For instance, begin the letter, "Dear Judge Dan." Then tell Judge Dan how you feel about his presence in you and how you intend to relate with him in the future. Ask any questions that you might have about why he is present within you.

3. As a closure to this meditation, compose a prayer asking God to give you the wisdom to know this aspect of yourself and the courage to deal with it.

Memory Verse

Take this verse with you in your heart and on your lips:

> Righteous art thou, O Lord,
>   and right are thy judgments.

(Ps. 119:137)

BETH: *The Book of Genesis begins with the letter* beth, *as in* bereshith *or "beginning." "In the beginning God created . . ." The birth of Moses is the beginning of a new era for the Hebrew people, enslaved in Egypt.* Beth *also stands for* binah, *or "understanding." Moses will be given a new and deeper understanding of God's words and commandments.*

Awakening to New Life

This meditation on birth and new life is an invitation to awaken to new life, especially during times of distress. As seen in meditation 1, conditions are getting worse for the Israelites. Taskmasters have been set over them to force them to build the cities of Pithom and Raamses. The Hebrew names of these cities—meaning "narrow place" and "son of the sun," respectively—point to the confining and idolatrous conditions to which the Israelites are reduced. Yet even a situation like this is not without hope. Life does come out of death. Seeds are nurtured in the darkness. The sun does shine even before it rises.

Become aware of the confinement and idolatry in your own life. Then read the following passage and enter into the historical narrative. Read the passage again, but this time read it as your own story. In the midst of the slavery and bondage that may be part of your life, "hear" the invitation to be reborn and awakened to new life.

Exodus 2:1–10

Now a man from the house of Levi went and took to wife a daughter of Levi. The woman conceived and bore a son; and when she saw that he was a goodly child, she hid him three months. And when she could hide him no longer she took for him a basket made of bulrushes, and daubed it with bitumen and pitch; and she put the child in it and placed it among the reeds at the river's brink. And his sister stood at a distance, to know what would be done to him. Now the daughter of Pharaoh came down to bathe at the river, and her maidens walked beside the river; she saw the basket among the reeds and sent her maid to fetch it. When she opened it she saw the child; and lo, the babe was crying. She took pity on him and said, "This is one of the Hebrews' children." Then his sister said to Pharaoh's daughter, "Shall I go and call you a nurse from the Hebrew women to nurse the child for you?" And Pharaoh's daughter said to her, "Go." So the girl went and called the child's mother. And Pharaoh's daughter said to her, "Take this child away, and nurse him for me, and I will give you your wages." So the woman took the child and nursed him. And the child grew, and she brought him to Pharaoh's daughter, and he became her son; and she named him Moses, for she said, "Because I drew him out of the water."

Commentary

This scriptural reading reveals the miraculous power of the Divine Presence in the miracle of birth. The parents of Moses are identified in Exod. 6:20 as Amram and Jochebed. *Amram* means "kindred of the most high" and *Jochebed*, "divine splendor." These are people touched by God. When the Divine touches Creation, miracles occur: "The woman conceived and bore a son."

The child born is called "goodly," not only possessing natural beauty but also enveloped in the extraordinary beauty of the Divine Presence, which fills the house.

Pharaoh has ordered that all male Hebrew babies be killed. So Jochebed risks her own life and that of the whole household to save the newborn child's life. After three months, when she can no longer hide him safely in the house, she puts the newborn in God's trust, placing him in a watertight basket afloat on the Nile River. Miriam, the child's sister, stations herself by the river and waits—life waiting upon life.

When Pharaoh's daughter comes to the Nile to bathe, she sees the basket among the reeds and sends her slave girl to fetch it. It is a tense moment. Will the newborn life be handed over to be killed, or will it be protected to go on living?

The princess opens the basket. The cries of the child touch her heart, moving her to pity. Defying her father's orders, she hires a wet nurse, who, unknown to her, is the child's mother.

Is this act anything more than an act of human kindness? Is the princess being "prompted" to act on the child's behalf? Rashi, a leading biblical commentator of the eleventh century, suggested that when Pharaoh's daughter opens the basket, she sees not only the child but also the glory of the Lord shining upon him. Awed and inspired by the miracle of this child, she acts to save him.

God's plan for Moses includes the selection of his mother as the wet nurse. God's will is done, even when the participants are unaware of it.

The name assigned to Pharaoh's daughter by tradition is *Bithiah*, which can be translated as "daughter of God." Even though this woman is Pharaoh's daughter of Egyptian origin, her obedience to the divine voice makes her a beloved daughter of God. She is the woman who gives the name *Moses* to the future lawgiver and prophet of Israel.

The drama played through and with women in the first two chapters of Exodus is remarkable. Israel's women are fertile; their fertility is Pharaoh's concern and target. His plans to destroy Israel are countered by the midwives, Shiphrah and Puah, by Miriam and Jochebed, and even by his own daughter, Bithiah. Israel was redeemed because of its righteous women.

These scriptural passages commemorate for posterity not only the role of women but also the importance of a child. In the first ten verses of chapter 2 of Exodus, the word *child* (*yeledh*) occurs seven times. There can be no doubt about the importance of the child and the care that is to be lavished upon him. This should apply to every child we meet, including the child that is buried deep within each one of us.

In the conception, birth, protection, and growth of a child, the miraculous is evident. For those with eyes to see, the miraculous is everywhere. The psalmist declared it:

> The heavens are telling the glory of God;
> and the firmament proclaims [thy] handiwork.
>
> (Ps. 19:1)

Mystics have recognized it, as well as poets:

> i thank You God for most this amazing
> day:for the leaping greenly spirits of trees
> and a blue true dream of sky;and for everything
> which is natural which is infinite which is yes
>
> (e. e. cummings, *100 Selected Poems*, p. 114)

The divine hand is everywhere to be found, the divine voice always to be heard, and the divine summons constantly to be received and obeyed.

Reflection and Journal-writing Exercises

The account of the birth of Moses is a description of conception and birth in your own life. The Divine Lover is God. The seed is every word that comes from the mouth of God. The Moses within you is the gift from God that will lead you out of bondage. The Jochebed within you nourishes and protects your Moses, and Miriam watches with care. The Bithiah within you defies your Pharaoh out of compassion for life.

• To hear and receive the word of God, sit quietly, comfortable and relaxed. A moment of slow and deep breathing will help you do this. Allow your mind to reflect on the three significant periods of your life: childhood, youth, and adulthood.

• Recall an episode from each period, a time of birth and growth. It might be a feeling you had of being set adrift alone on the waters of life, a time when events were out of your control and all you could do was wait, or a time when you risked speaking a word of love or asking for forgiveness. As you reflect, try using your ears rather than your eyes, for the ear is considered the most important organ of the human body and the word *hear* the most important command (Deut. 6:4). Let the scriptural story speak to you.

• Note each of these episodes in your journal.

• Take one of the three episodes and listen to it anew; feel it again; ask God that you might become aware of the Divine in it; and ask where you are being led by it now.

• Dialogue with Jochebed, Miriam, Bithiah, or Moses about this episode of new life. For instance, you can talk with Jochebed about how you nourished and protected this episode so that it could come to fulfillment. Or with Moses you could discuss the prophetic elements that were manifest in the episode. Ask for his advice about how you can continue to be led out of bondage to new life.

• Recount, question, and answer such issues as what resistance you gave to the episode of birth or growth, what miraculous elements were present, what or who helped you to gain new life or to grow, what God was trying to say to you through and in it all, and where should you move with it now.

In all of this, trust that God is present in the awakening to new life.

Memory Verse

Take this verse with you in your heart and on your lips:

> Blessed be thou, O Lord;
>   teach me thy statutes!
>
>   (Ps. 119:12)

GIMEL: Gimel *stands for* Gershom, *the son of Moses and Zipporah.* Gershom *means "a stranger in a strange land," the state, at one time or another, of all pilgrims.* Gimel *has a foot extended to the left, which stands for action. Moses moves to rescue his brothers and sisters.*

Change and Upheaval

The first ten verses of chapter 2 of Exodus describe Moses' childhood. The next twelve verses deal with his passage from childhood to adulthood and offer us an insight into the shaping of human character. The passage is filled with change and upheaval. Moses loses everything he has: his privileges, his life of ease, his honor. Yet through it all he is growing in wisdom and understanding, and at the end of this passage, a new life and a new home are offered to him.

As you read the scriptural passage, note the main events of Moses' transformation from a youthful prince in Pharaoh's court to a refugee in Midian. Mark the points at which Moses could refuse to go forward, the risks he takes, and the courage he displays.

Read the passage a second time, conscious of your own growth from childhood to adulthood. Recall the events that forced you to grow. Remember that the most painful times are often the moments of greatest growth. It is possible to encapsulate several years of your life in a few major events.

Exodus 2:11–22

One day, when Moses had grown up, he went out to his people and looked on their burdens; and he saw an Egyptian beating a Hebrew, one of his people. He looked this way and that, and seeing no one he killed the Egyptian and hid him in the sand. When he went out the next day, behold, two Hebrews were struggling together; and he said to the man that did the wrong, "Why do you strike your fellow?" He answered, "Who made you a prince and a judge over us? Do you mean to kill me as you killed the Egyptian?" Then Moses was afraid, and thought, "Surely the thing is known." When Pharaoh heard of it, he sought to kill Moses.

But Moses fled from Pharaoh, and stayed in the land of Midian; and he sat down by a well. Now the priest of Midian had seven daughters; and they came and drew water, and filled the troughs to water their father's flock. The shepherds came and drove them away; but Moses stood up and helped them, and watered their flock. When they came to their father Reuel, he said, "How is it that you have come so soon today?" They said, "An Egyptian delivered us out of the hand of the shepherds, and even drew water for us and watered the flock." He said to his daughters, "And where is he? Why have you left the man? Call him, that he may eat bread." And Moses was content to dwell with the man, and he gave Moses his daughter Zipporah. She bore a son, and he called his name Gershom; for he said, "I have been a sojourner in a foreign land."

Commentary

We journeyed with Moses through the events that brought him to Pharaoh's court. As a prince of the court, he is initiated into the liberal arts and sciences, the kind of education needed for a leader of people. During the years of Moses' training at court, the oppression of his people increases. Moses does not yet know the extent of this oppression, nor does he know that he is to be called by God to deliver the people from bondage.

The beginning of the day of reckoning arrives. Moses leaves the court and tours Pharaoh's kingdom. His eyes are opened to oppression and its consequences. First he sees an Egyptian beating a Hebrew. Unable to contain himself, he kills the Egyptian and hides him in the sand, hoping his action will not be discovered. Next he sees two Hebrews fighting one another and, in his attempt to make peace, only angers the offender, who reveals that they know of Moses' killing the Egyptian and have reported him to Pharaoh.

Moses is horrified that he has been found out. He was trying to help his people, and his first pursuit of justice ended in betrayal. Two of his own people have reported him to Pharaoh. Their names are Dathan and Abiram, which together mean "refusal to repent."

How quickly things change! One minute, Moses is an honorable prince in Pharaoh's court, and the next minute he is a fugitive fleeing for his life. The secure and assured prince has become a man knowing failure and deception.

Trials like this are not unknown to those who set out on the spiritual journey. In a short time, in an instant, a secure, comfortable life can be changed into one of doubt and insecurity. In these times of adversity, people are always tempted to look back and try to regain the good things of the past.

We cannot help but wonder if Moses regrets the day he became involved. Does he wish that he had remained at court, where he was one of the privileged and could have forgotten his poor beginnings and his people serving as slaves in Pharaoh's work force? Life could have been so much easier for him, even if less exciting and dramatic. But it is too late now for Moses to look back; that door is closed to him forever.

Moses flees and arrives in the land of Midian, where he will be trained and tested further. (The name *Midian* stands for a land of "striving and judgment.") It must have taken him days and even months to travel that distance. What happened to him during that time? How many desolate hours did he have? How many times was he close to death from hunger, thirst, and cold? What questions and doubts arose in his mind? What dreams did he have? The biblical text answers none of these questions. We can only imagine what it must have been like for him to wander through the wilderness on his own.

Moses sits down beside a well, which is a symbol of truth and nourishment. He is unaware that he is about to begin a time of rest and respite. He is simply sitting by the well when he is aroused by the screams of women being mistreated by shepherds, who push the women and their flock away in order to water their own flock. Not having lost his passion for justice, Moses rises up, defends the women, and waters their flock for them.

This is the third time that Moses has come to the aid of someone in trouble. The quarrel this time does not involve Hebrews but is between groups of people who are strangers to him. This makes no difference. Moses knows no distinction between person and person, only between right and wrong being done to another human being. Fidelity to justice in this instance brings a series of new events that lead to Moses' receiving a home, a wife, a family, and the pastoral care of sheep owned by Jethro (who is also called Reuel).

Sometimes the results of fidelity are hard to predict, and harder to understand. They may include leaving a comfortable life, exchanging the known for the unknown, success for failure, security for insecurity. The paradox is that such consequences seem necessary for the strengthening and maturing of the human spirit.

As one test is passed, a new way is opened. However, the old way is not left behind completely, as is demonstrated in Moses' being identified as an Egyptian. Like him, we still use the "persona" of our upbringing and still wear masks of former days, but our authentic self becomes more visible as the refining process continues.

Support for the journey is always available when most critically needed, though not always immediately recognized. For Moses this support is Jethro, a spiritual person. We too have supports and guides to help us enter new areas, encounter new obstacles, and face ever more exacting conditions. Like Moses, during some moments in our life, our main task is simply to receive and to be nourished by others.

Moses is content to stay with Jethro and his daughters. He marries one of the daughters, Zipporah, and they have a son, who is named Gershom; this name means "a stranger in a strange land." The name and the naming indicate that for Moses, the time for rest is temporary. The journey will continue. The fulfillment of his destiny is yet to come.

Reflection and Journal-writing Exercises

1. Moses' journey to adulthood begins when he leaves the court family, never again to return to it as one of its members. His first exercise of freedom results in failure (or is it a blessing?) and causes him to flee for his life. When he finally arrives in Midian, he is ready to begin a new life and to meet new challenges. *Gershom,* the name of his first son, describes the point of the journey at which he has arrived—"a stranger in a strange land."

When we pass from childhood to adulthood, we make a journey similar to that of Moses. Like his journey, ours includes movement from dependence to independence, from passivity to self-assertion. The umbilical cord from the natural or surrogate mother is cut, the loneliness of independence is faced, and the responsibility of freedom is assumed. Like Moses, we might not know that we are responding to a higher call. Perhaps all we know is that we must go, we must change, even though the passage is not easy and the future is uncertain.

• In your journal, write out a conversation between yourself and one of the biblical characters in this meditation. Discuss your transition from childhood to adulthood. If you have made a major change in your life or are beginning to feel that you should make one, Moses is a good dialogue partner. If your life involves no change of locale but has changed radically or may change radically through the entrance of an unexpected character or event, Zipporah will understand you. If you feel alienated and alone because of life-changing events that have preceded you, talk to Gershom, who was born in the desert. If your transition involves a struggle with evil, ask Moses what to do with the Dathans and Abirams who are afflicting you.

- If you prefer, your dialogue partner could be an event, an experience, or a value. For example, you could give death, separation, or wisdom personal attributes and image it as a person with whom you can converse.

2. When you have completed your dialogue, summarize what you have learned and offer it as a prayer of thanksgiving to God.

Memory Verse

Take this verse with you in your heart and on your lips:

I am a sojourner on earth;
    hide not thy commandments from me!

(Ps. 119:19)

MEDITATION 4

DALET: Dalet *stands for* deleth, *"door," and* derakhym, *"ways." Moses finds the door that will open the way for him to save his people.*

An Encounter with God

Moses has made a long journey both outwardly and inwardly. He has traveled from Egypt to Midian, from childhood to adulthood, from being a self-seeking child to being a compassionate human being—able to weep with others in their suffering and to risk his life for their welfare. Yet until now, Moses does not seem to have had a spiritual awakening. He is not aware that all along he has been called, invited, protected, and challenged by One whose name he does not know and of whose existence he is not conscious. He is unaware that his fidelity to himself is fidelity to God.

The time for meeting this God is at hand. Moses' journey has prepared him. It is a moment of encounter for which God has been waiting, and after it neither Moses nor the world will ever be the same again.

As you continue your journey with these verses of the Scriptures, let Moses' encounter with God and his awakening to the Divine in his life be a revelation of your own encounter with God and a further awakening to the Divine in your life.

Exodus 2:23—3:10

In the course of those many days the king of Egypt died. And the people of Israel groaned under their bondage, and cried out for help, and their cry under bondage came up to God. And *God heard* their groaning, and *God remembered* [the] covenant with Abraham, with Isaac, and with Jacob. And *God saw* the people of Israel, and *God knew* their condition.

Now Moses was keeping the flock of his father-in-law, Jethro, the priest of Midian; and he led his flock to the west side of the wilderness, and came to Horeb, the mountain of God. And the angel of the LORD appeared to him in a flame of fire out of the midst of a bush; and he looked, and lo, the bush was burning, yet it was not consumed. And Moses said, "I will turn aside and see this great sight, why the bush is not burnt." When the LORD saw that he turned aside to see, God called to him out of the bush, "Moses, Moses!" And he said, "Here am I." Then [God] said, "Do not come near; put off your shoes from your feet, for the place on which you are standing is holy ground." And [God] said, "I am the God of your [ancestors], the God of Abraham, the God of Isaac, and the God of Jacob." And Moses hid his face, for he was afraid to look at God.

Then the LORD said, "I have seen the affliction of my people who are in Egypt, and have heard their cry because of their taskmasters; I know their sufferings, and I have come down to deliver them out of the hand of the Egyptians, and to bring them up out of that land to a good and broad land, a land flowing with milk and honey, to the place of the Canaanites, the Hittites, the Amorites, the Perizzites, the Hivites, and the Jebusites. And now, behold, the cry of the people of Israel has come to me, and I have seen the oppression with which the Egyptians oppress them. Come, I will send you to Pharaoh that you may bring forth my people, the [children] of Israel, out of Egypt." (Emphasis added.)

Commentary

The last three verses of chapter 2 of Exodus are included as part
of the scriptural portion for this meditation because these verses
form an important literary bridge connecting the prologue of
chapters 1 and 2 with the story of redemption that begins in
chapter 3.

Up to this point in the biblical narrative, no direct reference
to God (except in connection with the midwives) has been
made. This seems strange. Where was God during all this time?
Did God abandon the people? Or did the people abandon God?
Did God not promise Jacob, "'I will go down with you to Egypt,
and I will also bring you up again . . .'" (Gen. 46:4)?

The Scriptures portray the people as having abandoned
God. By not mentioning God in the first two chapters of Exodus, the biblical writer used a literary device to indicate that the
Israelites no longer remember God. When did this forgetfulness
begin? When life was secure and they had few needs? Is forget-
ting God the cause of their bondage, or is their bondage the
cause of their forgetfulness? It appears to work both ways.
When people forget the God of their ancestors, they lose their
identity and spirit and easily fall into bondage. And the
bondage itself can have a numbing and dulling effect that
blocks out the memory of God and of God's promises.

Whatever the cause of God's seeming absence, a radical
change is in the making. The people, groaning in their pain, cry
out for help. *God hears* their groaning; *God remembers* the
covenant made with Abraham and Sarah, Isaac and Rebekah, Jacob and Rachel; *God sees* the people of Israel; and *God knows* of
their condition. The Scriptures' fourfold repetition of the name
God, each followed by a verb indicating progressively intimate
God-responses, points dramatically to a growing reappearance
of God in the lives of the people of Israel and a progressive
breaking down of barriers that separate God and the people:
God hears; God remembers; God sees; and God knows.

In Midian, Moses is tending his father-in-law's sheep. From
shepherding, Moses has learned how to lead a group of creatures who panic easily. He now knows the desert and its ways
and the seasons with their changing moods. He has become acquainted with silence and the sounds of silence around and

within himself. Not only has he watered sheep at the well of Jethro, but he has been watered from a well deep inside himself.

Moses leads his flock to the west side of the wilderness, to Horeb, the mountain of God. *Horeb* means "solitude," "desolation," a state of being prior to a mystical experience. Moses takes the sheep to the edge of the desert, a remote place where one is not likely to be disturbed or interrupted.

While Moses watches his flock feeding, he is startled by a bush burning with a fire that does not consume the bush. As Moses stops to look, he hears God's voice, "'Moses, Moses!'" Startled, Moses replies, "'Here am I.'" The voice commands, "'Do not come near; put off your shoes from your feet, for the place on which you are standing is holy ground.'" Moses removes his shoes. The voice continues, "I am the God of your ancestors, of Abraham and Sarah, of Isaac and Rebekah, of Jacob and Leah and Rachel." Stunned and overcome, Moses hides his face, for he is afraid to look at God.

Up to this moment, Moses has not met God, but now he is ready. Stopping, looking, listening, and marveling with a reverent fear are the responses of a person ready to encounter the Divine.

Moses is called twice by name: "'Moses, Moses!'" There is a sense of urgency on God's part. The time has come for deliverance. The repetition of Moses' name also tells us something about Moses. Being called by name indicates the recognition by the caller of the uniqueness and specialness of the one called. In God's eyes, Moses is not just anyone. He is Moses. He is an individual. Moses is no longer a child. He is a mature adult, ready to be called and sent forth.

Moses responds, "'Here am I,'" and the deepening of intimacy continues. At God's command, Moses takes off his sandals as one on the threshold of the house of another. Moses is standing on holy ground, at a holy moment, in the presence of the Holy One. Like a lover, he is caught up in the Beloved. In the rapture of the moment, he is ready to trust himself to God's will.

The trust is reciprocal. God counts on Moses: "'I have seen the affliction of my people. . . . Come, I will send you to Pharaoh.'"

Reflection and Journal-writing Exercises

1. When we try to describe an encounter with God—or with anyone—logic, reason, and ordinary language fail us. We need to use images and symbols in order to recapture the experience. We need poetry and song. For this reason, use your imagination in this exercise.

• Imagine yourself in a desert—a remote place on the edge of the wilderness. Vast, trackless wasteland spreads out before you and behind you. You are alone with your doubts and questions that have no answers. Your mouth is dry with dust. Your feet hurt from the confinement of your shoes, and your soul is as cold as the night air.

   Suddenly, without warning, you are standing before the burning bush. The cold darkness is pushed back, and a warm cloud of light wraps itself around you. You hear a voice calling your name. Your name is repeated. The tone of the voice moves you deeply. At first you cannot speak. Then you reply, "Speak, Lord. Your servant is listening." You listen intently to hear a voice that is faint at the beginning but getting louder and clearer as you listen. What is God calling you to do or be? Is God calling you to lead someone or yourself out of bondage?

2. If at first nothing seems to happen in exercise 1, journey with the imagery a second time. This time take off your shoes, perhaps at the point when you realize how confining they are. Let the feeling of your bared feet touch off a new openness to and reverence for God. Rest patiently in God's presence, responding as you feel called to respond.

3. In your journal, write to yourself about this experience. It might be in the writing that God's voice is heard.

Memory Verse

Take this verse with you in your heart and on your lips:

> Make me understand the way of thy precepts,
>   and I will meditate on thy wondrous works.
>   (Ps. 119:27)

MEM: Mem *has two forms. The open* מ *is used anywhere in a word except at the end, where the closed* ם *is used. Figuratively, the open* mem *stands for the openly revealed actions of God, and the closed* mem *alludes to God's activity that is yet hidden from human eyes as well as to divine protection. Moses experiences both God's revelation and God's divine protection.*

Setting Out Again

The difficulty we have in believing in our worth and in performing the noble tasks God demands of us is also a chapter of Moses' life journey. When facing the sobering reality of God's call, Moses is reluctant to say yes. He gives every imaginable excuse to evade such demands. For every excuse that Moses makes, God gives an answer. But Moses does not want God's answers. He simply wants to be left alone.

The drama intensifies as we wonder whether Moses will take the leap of faith that moves one from the rapture of an encounter with God to a mission of service. On his answer rests the fate of the Israelites and that of the whole world.

Read the following text twice as you try to enter into Moses' interior conflict. Read it again as you reflect on critical moments of decision-making in your own life.

Exodus 3:9—4:15

"And now, behold, the cry of the people of Israel has come to me, and I have seen the oppression with which the Egyptians oppress them. Come, I will send you to Pharaoh that you may bring forth my people, the [children] of Israel, out of Egypt." But Moses said to God, "Who am I that I should go to Pharaoh, and bring the [children] of Israel out of Egypt?" [God] said, "But I will be with you; and this shall be the sign for you, that I have sent you: when you have brought forth the people out of Egypt, you shall serve God upon this mountain."

Then Moses said to God, "If I come to the people of Israel and say to them, 'The God of your [ancestors] has sent me to you,' and they ask me, 'What is [God's] name?' what shall I say to them?" God said to Moses, "I AM WHO I AM." And [God] said, "Say this to the people of Israel, 'I AM has sent me to you.'" God also said to Moses, "Say this to the people of Israel, 'The LORD, the God of your [ancestors] . . . has sent me to you': this is my name for ever, and thus I am to be remembered throughout all generations. Go and gather the elders of Israel together and say to them, 'The LORD, the God of your [ancestors] . . . has appeared to me, saying, "I have observed you and what has been done to you in Egypt; and I promise that I will bring you up out of the affliction of Egypt to . . . a land flowing with milk and honey."'. . ."

Then Moses answered, "But behold, they will not believe me or listen to my voice, for they will say, 'The LORD did not appear to you.'" The LORD said to him, "What is that in your hand?" He said, "A rod." And [God] said, "Cast it on the ground." So he cast it on the ground, and it became a serpent; and Moses fled from it. But the LORD said to Moses, "Put out your hand, and take it by the tail"—so he put out his hand and caught it, and it became a rod in his hand—"that they may believe that the LORD, the God of their [ancestors] . . . has appeared to you.". . .

But Moses said to the LORD, "Oh, my Lord, I am not eloquent, either heretofore or since thou hast spoken to thy servant; but I am slow of speech and of tongue." Then the

LORD said to him, "Who has made [your] mouth? Who makes [people] dumb, or deaf, or seeing, or blind? Is it not I, the LORD? Now therefore go, and I will be with your mouth and teach you what you shall speak." But he said, "Oh, my Lord, send, I pray, some other person." Then the anger of the LORD was kindled against Moses and [God] said, "Is there not Aaron, your brother, the Levite? I know that he can speak well; and behold, he is coming out to meet you, and when he sees you he will be glad in his heart. And you shall speak to him and put the words in his mouth; and I will be with your mouth and with his mouth, and will teach you what you shall do."

Commentary

The scriptural conversation between God and Moses rests upon God's command, Moses' doubts, and God's promises. The exchange reveals much about God and the lengths to which God will go to move humans to freely participate in the divine will. In the conversation Moses neither hides nor denies his doubts. However, human doubts and reluctance do not deter God. Rather than a reprimand, Moses receives two important revelations: God's name and the promise "I will be with you."

God reveals the divine name to Moses as *Eheyeh-Asher-Eheyeh*. The Hebrew word *Eheyeh* comes from the verb "to be," but it is not clear what tense it is in. So the name has been variously translated as "I AM WHO I AM"; "I WILL BE WHO I WILL BE"; and "I AM WHO I WILL BE." Each of these translations indicates that the name of God is anything but static.

God's self-definition changes, as it were, according to our response to God's self-disclosure and involvement in our life. "I WILL BE WHO I WILL BE" can read, "I will be for you who I will be according to your response to me." Apparently God accommodates to human strength and weaknesses, allowing our positive strengths to function while making up for our weaknesses.

The initial impact of Moses' encounter with God seems to lose force, and continued assurances are needed to counter his doubts and reluctance. Before and after the revelation of the name, God assures Moses, "I will be with you."

Three times within a few verses God makes the promise of the accompanying divine presence. The first time Moses hesitates to assent to the divine summons, God says, "'I will be with you.'" When Moses complains about his bumbling speech, God assures him, "'I will be with your mouth and teach you what you shall speak.'" Three verses further, the same promise is made, but this time not only to Moses but to Aaron as well: "'And you shall speak to [Aaron] and put the words in his mouth; and I will be with your mouth and with his mouth, and will teach you what you shall do.'" Relentlessly, God encourages and assures Moses.

God's promises also reveal that the mission Moses is sent to accomplish is God's mission. Its success is assured. But what about Moses? To what extent will he continue to believe these promises and remain faithful, especially when the road gets rough and begins to twist back and forth? When the way is unclear and the end not yet in sight? What more will God do to lead Moses on the journey to freedom?

Reflection and Journal-writing Exercises

In this meditation you need to get in touch with your own personal call from God and your own doubts and hesitations. Like Moses, express your doubts and listen to God's assurances of "I will be with you." One or both of the following suggestions may help you in this endeavor:

1. Think of an episode in your life during which you have felt called by God to do something. Write out a conversation with God that follows the manner in which God and Moses conversed. Express God's call, your doubts, and God's answers to your doubts.

2. Imagine yourself resting in your room after a tiring day of work. You are just dozing off to sleep when you hear a knock at the door. You open your eyes and notice that the room is brighter than usual. As you rub the sleep from your eyes, the door swings open on its hinges. A gust of wind sweeps by. You

hear a voice calling you by name, not once but twice. Using your imagination, allow the scene to develop. Let your pen flow with your imagination. Again, let the story of Moses and God inspire your story of God and yourself.

Memory Verse

Take this verse with you in your heart and on your lips:

> I understand more than the aged,
>   for I keep thy precepts.
>   (Ps. 119:100)

MEDITATION 6

VAV: *The letter* vav, *upright and unadorned, stands for truth. The word* vav *literally means "a connective hook" and joins words and phrases together. This connecting function is appropriate for the letter of truth because all truth ultimately leads to unity and harmony.*

Moment of Hesitation

In meditation 5, Moses made every possible excuse to evade the demands of God. In the end, though, God's promises prevailed: "Go, I will be with you." Moses ran out of excuses, and according to the biblical text, he said nothing more. He now goes to his father-in-law, Jethro, to tell him that he must return to Egypt. Moses leaves the security of his newly established household and sets out on the journey back to Egypt. New dangers threaten his life, yet he cannot turn back. In the face of uncertainties, moved by the divine promise "I will be with you," Moses is determined to go on.

While reading the scriptural passage, allow yourself to experience the mixture of events and feelings that Moses is experiencing. Remember that he is following what he believes to be God's call. How does he feel when Jethro seems to understand his leaving the family household? What emotions surge through him after his close brush with death? What goes on in his heart when he meets Aaron and when they stand before Pharaoh?

Exodus 4:18—5:1

Moses went back to Jethro his father-in-law and said to him, "Let me go back, I pray, to my [kinsfolk] in Egypt and see whether they are still alive." And Jethro said to Moses, "Go in peace." . . . So Moses took his wife and his sons and set them on an ass, and went back to the land of Egypt; and in his hand Moses took the rod of God. . . .

At a lodging place on the way the LORD met him and sought to kill him. Then Zipporah took a flint and cut off her son's foreskin, and touched Moses' feet with it, and said, "Surely you are a bridegroom of blood to me!" So [God] let him alone. Then it was that she said, "You are a bridegroom of blood," because of the circumcision.

The LORD said to Aaron, "Go into the wilderness to meet Moses." So he went, and met him at the mountain of God and kissed him. And Moses told Aaron all the words of the LORD with which [the LORD] had sent him, and all the signs which [the LORD] had charged him to do. Then Moses and Aaron went and gathered together all the elders of the people of Israel. And Aaron spoke all the words which the LORD had spoken to Moses, and did the signs in the sight of the people. And the people believed; and when they heard that the LORD had visited the people of Israel and that [the LORD] had seen their affliction, they bowed their heads and worshiped.

Afterward Moses and Aaron went to Pharaoh and said, "Thus says the LORD, the God of Israel, 'Let my people go, that they may hold a feast to me in the wilderness.'"

Commentary

When Moses decides that he must leave his household in Midian and return to Egypt, he goes to his father-in-law, Jethro, to get his permission. We can imagine Moses' perplexity as he thinks of ways to explain to his father-in-law why he and his family must set out on this strange journey. He knows that it will be difficult for Jethro to part with his daughter and his grandchildren. Yet Jethro says, "'Go in peace.'" Other biblical texts say that Jethro is a religious man, so we can assume that he recognizes the mystery of the Divine at work in Moses' decision to leave. Moses says good-bye to this stage of his life and sets his face to the future.

Moses' family travels on an ass. The ass is an important animal in the Scriptures. It was present when Abraham set out with his son, Isaac, for a mountain in the land of Moriah (Gen. 22:1–14). The same animal is standing ready now to accompany Moses and his wife and children to Egypt. Later, it will carry the pregnant Mary, accompanied by her husband, Joseph, to Bethlehem. According to Hebrew tradition, the ass, although considered one of the most ignorant animals, will know of the Messiah's arrival when he comes.

In addition, the ass is an important symbol on a personal level. It stands for a sensory instinct that often is moved and stirred by the presence of God before our intellect realizes what is happening. Our bodily senses are able to alert us to the presence of the Divine. The respect that the Scriptures give to the ass is symbolic of the respect due to our own body, which has been fashioned by the hand of God and is sensitive to the presence of our Maker.

On the way, Moses and Zipporah stop for the night at a lodging place, where they have a bewildering experience. Moses is attacked by a divine agent. The episode is similar to the one experienced by Jacob (Gen. 32:24–32). In both cases, the men are travelers commissioned by God when they encounter a spirit that tries to kill them. Martin Buber, a Jewish scholar and philosopher, tried to explain such a moment in the life of a scriptural hero:

> We know from the life of the founders of religions . . . that there is such an "event of the night"; the sudden collapse of the newly-won certainty, the "deadly factual" moment when the demon working with apparently unbounded authority appears in the world where God alone had been in control but a moment before. . . . In the account of the manner in which YHVH meets Moses as a demon . . . is the unmistakable language of a tradition which also points to the obscure yet perceptible threshold of experience. (*Moses*, pp. 58–59)

Zipporah saves Moses' life by circumcising one of their sons. We are not sure why this act saves his life. Perhaps it serves as a ritual reminder of God's covenant with Moses' ancestors and as a concrete recommitment by Moses to that covenant.

Zipporah's protection of Moses is indicative of the help Moses will receive throughout his mission. When God commissions a task, divine assistance is provided in many ways, often unrecognized as such. Stories illustrating this fill the Bible. When God commissions us to do a task, we can be certain that we will not be left alone, even though it may seem so at times. Of course, the help that God intends can be rejected or forestalled. For instance, when Moses and Aaron assemble the elders, repeat all the words that the Lord has spoken to Moses, and perform the signs in the sight of the people, the elders become convinced and are supportive. Yet Moses and Aaron seemingly go to Pharaoh alone. Why only Moses and Aaron? God had told Moses, "'Go and gather the elders of Israel together, . . . and you and the elders of Israel shall go to the king of Egypt . . .'" (Exod. 3:16–18).

What happened? We can only imagine what the elders think and say. For example, "If God spoke, why did God not speak to us, the leaders of the people? Who is this Moses anyway? Was he not the one who had to flee the country because he murdered an Egyptian? Did he not try to make himself our leader before? If we listen to him, we will all be destroyed. What chance have we, oppressed slaves that we are, to defy Pharaoh and his armies? Better to leave good enough alone."

Jealousy, resentment, fear, and apathy—whether in ourselves or in others—can reject and forestall the support God has prepared.

Reflection and Journal-writing Exercises

1. The commanding voice of God liberates. To obey God is to become free. This is a paradoxical principle that we do not understand and yet know to be true. If Moses obeys God and returns to Egypt, salvation will come to his people. If the Israelites obey God's command to leave Egypt, they will be liberated. God says, "'See, I have set before you this day life and good, death and evil. If you obey the commandments of the LORD your God which I command you this day, . . . you shall live. . . . But if your heart turns away, and you will not hear . . . you shall perish . . .'" (Deut. 30:15–18).

- Note in your journal any episode in your life when you have experienced this paradox.

2. Struggle is a condition of growth. The human person is sometimes a battleground for the conflicting forces of good and evil. Unless a person resists, that person will be overcome by evil. Moses' night encounter with death in the desert alerts him to dangers from his own rebellious nature and to dangers from without.

- Note in your journal a struggle with evil that you have experienced and write to Moses about it.

3. With God the impossible is possible. Some life tasks seem impossible. The task demanded of Moses seems to be one of these. Without the backing of the elders or his own people, without the support of an army and without weapons, Moses sets out to free the Israelites from Egypt. His only power is the power of obedience to the commanding voice of God.

- Note in your journal an achievement you have made that in the beginning seemed impossible.
- Recall the unforeseen occurrences that enabled the achievement.
- Note whether the achievement was exactly the way you originally intended it to be.

4. The following is a self-guided meditation requiring the use of your imagination. You can read this to yourself or record it on an audiotape and play it back to yourself. Do not force your imagination. Just let it move along the outlines of the narrative in such a way that your story will be unique to your life. Pause at the breaks indicated to give your imagination time to work.

- You are Moses at the site of the burning bush. . . . You would prefer to stay there and erect an altar or a monastery on the site. . . . But the voice of God commands you to go on. . . . You leave the spot even though you do not have all the answers and serious questions remain. . . . You are not long on your journey when conflicting emotions battle within you and voices bombard you from without. "Go back," they warn. . . . Frightened, you cry out to the Lord. . . . An angel appears and offers consolation. . . . Strengthened, you continue your journey. . . . You meet your brother, Aaron, who joins you. . . . Both of you appear before the elders of your people, who believe your message. . . . Just when you think that all is going well, everything collapses and you find yourself alone, commanded by God to do what is humanly impossible. . . . Yet you experience a strength that is new to you. It is conveyed by the words "Obey and I will be with you."

You may wish to record the details of your meditation experience in your journal.

Memory Verse

Take this verse with you in your heart and on your lips:

And take not the word of truth utterly out of my
   mouth. . . .

(Ps. 119:43)

GIMEL: *The letter* gimel *stands for "great"* (gadhol) *and "mighty"* (ghibor)—*the great and mighty God who empowers us to work for freedom and righteousness. The extended foot of* gimel *symbolizes action. God empowers us to act.*

Struggle for Freedom

At the end of meditation 6, Moses had arrived in Egypt to liberate the Israelites from the Egyptians. God's revelation, "that you may know that I am the LORD," is meant for all peoples. The Israelites, the Egyptians, the magicians, Pharaoh—all will come to know that God is the Lord. Yet Pharaoh does not want to know God and does not want to let others worship and adore this God either.

Part B focuses on the struggle for freedom that takes place. In meditation 7, we meet a Pharaoh who punishes the Israelites for wanting to serve and worship God and a Moses who is discouraged and complains to God that conditions for the people are becoming worse instead of better. God responds to Moses by revealing God's most intimate name and by empowering him with strength. In meditation 8, Moses, becoming a man who is powerful in word and deed, confronts Pharaoh and all his court, pitting the powers of good and evil against each other in a life-and-death struggle. The power of God is revealed through the plagues described in meditation 9, but Pharaoh's heart remains hardened. Good triumphs in meditation 10. Pharaoh, no longer wanting Moses and the Israelites in his country, drives them out; finally they are free to leave and to worship God. Moses begins to understand who God as "the Lord" is. Before beginning their journey across the sea and into the desert, Moses and the Israelites commemorate their deliverance in a Passover festival.

On a personal level, all of us are led to know who God as "the Lord" is. Like Moses, we have to confront the Pharaohs around and within us. The struggle is difficult as we are invited to make the break with enemies who do not want to know God. But finally, like Moses, empowered with the strength and perseverance that comes from knowing God in a new way and by a new name, we triumph over our enemies and are free to begin our journey to Mount Sinai.

LAMED: Lamed, *a majestic letter soaring above the other Hebraic letters, is like a town guardian in a lookout tower. The word* lamed *refers to learning and teaching, which, when focused on God's words, are two of the highest occupations of humans.*

Meeting the Enemy

The enemy, in the Scriptures, is anyone or anything that does not want to know God or God's will. Not surprisingly, Pharaoh, as the enemy, wants to know nothing of God. Yet God wants even Pharaoh—both the Pharaoh of Egypt and the Pharaoh within us—to know God, a God who is compassionate and merciful, a God who wills to save even the enemy.

Moses, who has already encountered God in the burning bush, is granted a further privilege in the revelation of God's most intimate name. Knowing this name, Moses is able to confront Pharaoh with renewed courage and determination.

Take a moment before reading the following scriptural passage to ask, "Who are you, Lord, that I should heed your voice?" When you are able to find some kind of answer to this question, proceed with the meditation, seeking further enlightenment.

Exodus 5:1— 6:2

Afterward Moses and Aaron went to Pharaoh and said, "Thus says the Lord, the God of Israel, 'Let my people go, that they may hold a feast to me in the wilderness.'" But Pharaoh said, "Who is the Lord, that I should heed [the voice of the Lord] and let Israel go? I do not know the Lord, and moreover I will not let Israel go." Then they said, "The God of the Hebrews has met with us; let us go, we pray, a three days' journey into the wilderness, and sacrifice to the Lord our God, lest [God] fall upon us with pestilence or with the sword." But the king of Egypt said to them, "Moses and Aaron, why do you take the people away from their work? Get to your burdens." And Pharaoh said, "Behold, the people of the land are now many and you make them rest from their burdens!" The same day Pharaoh commanded the taskmasters of the people and their foremen, "You shall no longer give the people straw to make bricks, as heretofore; let them go and gather straw for themselves. But the number of bricks which they made heretofore you shall lay upon them, you shall by no means lessen it; for they are idle; therefore they cry, 'Let us go and offer sacrifice to our God.' Let heavier work be laid upon the [people] that they may labor at it and pay no regard to lying words." . . .

. . . The foremen of the people of Israel saw that they were in evil plight, when they said, "You shall by no means lessen your daily number of bricks." They met Moses and Aaron, who were waiting for them, as they came forth from Pharaoh; and they said to them, "The Lord look upon you and judge, because you have made us offensive in the sight of Pharaoh and his servants, and have put a sword in their hand to kill us."

Then Moses turned again to the Lord, and said, "O Lord, why hast thou done evil to this people? Why didst thou ever send me? For since I came to Pharaoh to speak in thy name, he has done evil to this people, and thou hast not delivered thy people at all." But the LORD said to Moses, "Now you shall see what I will do to Pharaoh; for with a strong hand he will send them out, yea, with a strong hand he will drive them out of his land."

And God said to Moses, "I am the LORD."

Commentary

Moses and Aaron manage to get an audience with Pharaoh. When they do, they request that Pharaoh let the Israelites go to worship God. Pharaoh's response sets the main theme of the confrontation: "'Who is the LORD, that I should heed [the voice of the LORD] and let Israel go? I do not know the LORD, and moreover I will not let Israel go.'" Recognizing no power superior to his own, Pharaoh accuses Moses and Aaron of unsettling the Israelites, who seem to be resigned to their lot. Why stir them with ideas of freedom? To prevent any future requests for time to worship God, Pharaoh gives orders to further burden the Israelites with work.

Pharaoh is crafty. The more people are enslaved, the less conscious they are of their options, their rights as persons created by God. If a flicker of hope were sparked through the promise of redemption (a lie according to Pharaoh), it would soon be extinguished by the worsening conditions. Moreover, the increased labor will be construed as Moses' fault, not Pharaoh's.

Moses himself is shattered. His obedience to God has worsened the conditions of the people, not helped them. Moses turns to God accusingly, "'O LORD, why hast thou done evil to this people? Why didst thou ever send me? For since I came to Pharaoh to speak in thy name, he has done evil to this people, and thou hast not delivered thy people at all.'"

Who of us has not had a similar experience? Pharaoh, representing the part of us that refuses to believe in any supernatural reality and accepts only what can be physically experienced, asks, "Who is the Lord, that I should believe?" The Pharaoh within us refuses to believe that we are called to freedom from our attachment to possessions, familiar habits, and all the elements of our life that help us feel in control, even as they enslave us.

Just as God answers our wearied self, God answers Moses by reminding him, "'I am the LORD.'" God has many names, each revealing new dimensions of God's personality. We have heard some of the names, but we may not have heard all of them. Is it time to hear a new name? Five times in chapter 6 alone the phrase "'I am the LORD'" appears.

The name *Lord* appears in the Scriptures for the first time in the Genesis story of human creation: "then the LORD God formed [the earth creature] of dust from the ground, and breathed into [its] nostrils the breath of life . . ." (Gen. 2:7). In the account of the creation of nonhuman beings, God is revealed as a God of justice and order. But when God creates the human being, a creature possessing free will and in need of mercy, the attribute of mercy is revealed in the name *Lord*. God is the Lord God, the God of both justice and mercy.

The repetition of this name throughout the chapter is a clue to the message contained therein. At a time when Moses is discouraged, God is saying to him, "Do not forget that I am the Lord, a merciful and faithful God. I have heard the groaning of the children of Israel, and I have come to deliver them from the bondage of Egypt. Do not become discouraged and unbelieving. Although you have *heard* my name as Lord before, now you will *experience* me as Lord, the merciful and faithful One." Moses almost makes the same mistake that Pharaoh makes: Moses wants physical proof, immediately, that the Lord is powerful enough to save the chosen people.

To hear God revealing self as Lord should give Moses and the Israelites hope of true freedom, which is to become the people of God, a people with an identity, a worth, and a destiny of their own.

What is true for a nation is also true for individuals. When oppressed by a Pharaoh who does not want to know God, whether that Pharaoh is outside or within ourselves, we need to hear the name of God—a name that not only gives hope but shatters the control of the enemy. Oppressed persons need to hear that God is the Lord our God.

At this moment in their history, the Israelites are not ready to hear the name. They will not listen to Moses. They are still too unbelieving and their burdens are too heavy.

Reflection and Journal-writing Exercises

1. Prayerfully, spend some time with the following questions:
- How is the revelation of a God who is just and merciful threatening to Pharaoh? To the Pharaohs of today? To the Pharaoh within yourself?
- Which names of God most appeal to you? Which name do you most need to hear at this time of your life? Why is this name so appealing? Repeat the name over and over again, relishing the image of God that becomes present to you.

2. Think of a time when you refused to listen to the voice of the Lord, when some Pharaoh within you said, "I do not know the Lord."
- Relax and close your eyes. Let the scene of your refusal come vividly into your consciousness.
- Why did you resist recognizing the Lord? Was pride the cause? Did you fear the changes that this recognition would bring about?
- How did your Moses react? Did your hopeful and faithful Moses give up hope and faith? Did your Moses complain to God that God's backing had no tangible results? Pause again and ponder these questions.

3. Recall a time when the Lord somehow told you, "When all looks hopeless, I will come through in ways you never expected. I am the Lord."
- Did your Moses overcome your prideful and doubting Pharaoh?
- What was that experience like?
- Relax and let the images of the Lord supporting and upholding you be present.

4. Write in your journal any insights that have resulted from your reflections.

Memory Verse

Take this verse with you in your heart and on your lips:

> If thy law had not been my delight,
>   I should have perished in my affliction.
>
> (Ps. 119:92)

YOD: Yod *is a symbol used for both God and the human person. A single* yod *represents God, and two* yods *denote the human person.* Yod *also stands for* yad, *or "the hand of God." Moses is strengthened and empowered by God's hand.*

Empowered with Strength

In this meditation, you will witness the empowerment of Moses by God and an increasing hardening of Pharaoh's heart. Moses is given a power that makes him a formidable opponent of Pharaoh. This kind of power enables us to go beyond our ordinary abilities. It must be believed in and accepted. Rather than deny, because of false humility, that we possess power from God, we must claim it and be grateful for it. Ask the Lord now to help you recognize and accept this empowerment in your life.

Exodus 7:1–13

> And the LORD said to Moses, "See, I make you as God to Pharaoh; and Aaron your brother shall be your prophet. You shall speak all that I command you; and Aaron your brother shall tell Pharaoh to let the people of Israel go out of his land. But I will harden Pharaoh's heart, and though I multiply my signs and wonders in the land of Egypt, Pharaoh will not listen to you; then I will lay my hand

upon Egypt and bring forth my hosts, my people the [children] of Israel, out of the land of Egypt by great acts of judgment. And the Egyptians shall know that I am the LORD, when I stretch forth my hand upon Egypt and bring out the people of Israel from among them." And Moses and Aaron did so; they did as the LORD commanded them. Now Moses was eighty years old, and Aaron eighty-three years old, when they spoke to Pharaoh.

And the LORD said to Moses and Aaron, "When Pharaoh says to you, 'Prove yourselves by working a miracle,' then you shall say to Aaron, 'Take your rod and cast it down before Pharaoh, that it may become a serpent.'" So Moses and Aaron went to Pharaoh and did as the LORD commanded; Aaron cast down his rod before Pharaoh and his servants, and it became a serpent. Then Pharaoh summoned the wise men and the sorcerers; and they also, the magicians of Egypt, did the same by their secret arts. For every man cast down his rod, and they became serpents. But Aaron's rod swallowed up their rods. Still Pharaoh's heart was hardened, and he would not listen to them; as the LORD had said.

Commentary

Perhaps the most amazing words in this part of the Exodus story are "'See, I make you as God to Pharaoh.'" God is not simply using Moses; God is transforming him to be as God. In Moses, Pharaoh is encountering God. If Pharaoh rejects Moses, Pharaoh rejects God.

This kind of language has been used in the Scriptures before. In Genesis, each person is created in the image and likeness of God (Gen. 1:27). The knowledge of this likeness can be the source of temptation to evil as well as the source of empowerment for good. The serpent tempts Adam and Eve to supplant God, in whose image they are made. Is there a difference between being made like God—and witnessing this godlikeness to others—and trying to be God?

Apparently, although humans are made like God, contact with God or God's word makes humans even more godlike. The psalmist's prayer, "Thy word is a lamp to my feet and a light to my path," refers not only to the light that shines from God's word but also to the light that emanates from the person who receives and digests the word (Ps. 119:105). Later in the Exodus journey, when Moses comes down from Mount Sinai with the two tablets in his hand, the skin of his face shines with divine radiance (Exod. 34:29).

Even though Moses is already "as God," he will be godlike to Pharaoh only when Pharaoh recognizes it. God will need to prompt or inspire Pharaoh to see Moses for who he truly is—a god to Pharaoh. This interpretation is the one accepted by the following midrash:

> "Whatever God prompts any person or thing to do is described as [God's] 'command.' Reliable evidence of this interpretation is found in God's words to Moses, in [Exod. 6:30]: 'Behold I have made thee a god to Pharaoh' implying that I have inspired him with respect and awe of you and you will note it and rejoice." (Quoted in Nehama Leibowitz, *Studies in Shemot,* p. 143)

One day Pharaoh will recognize Moses as a god among his people. In the meantime, he does all in his power to close his eyes to the truth. Not wanting to behold the truth or to recognize God, Pharaoh's heart is hardened.

Why this hardening of Pharaoh's heart? Why does God harden his heart and then punish him? Is the God of Exodus truly a just God?

Created as persons with free will, people possess the power to choose between good and evil. If a person consistently chooses evil, that person becomes fixed or hardened in a position of no return. When this happens, we may say that God has stiffened or hardened that person's heart, meaning that God *allowed* the hardening of that person's heart.

On the other hand, "God's hardening of Pharaoh's heart" may be a literary way of dealing with what is beyond human comprehension. All of history, all of humankind, is ultimately under the power of God. Humans are not denied free choice, but they move only within the framework of God's design.

When Israel is freed from Egypt, it will not be because of Pharaoh or Moses but because of God: "'And the Egyptians shall know that I am the LORD, when I stretch forth my hand upon Egypt and bring out the people of Israel from among them.'"

Accompanying Pharaoh's hardening of heart is the work of his magicians, who, by performing spells, convince Pharaoh that the miracles wrought by Moses and Aaron are nothing extraordinary. Could the magicians' tricks symbolize those times when, reluctant to open up to God's voice, we use all kinds of rationalizations and distractions to ward it off? At times we are not certain which voice is God's and which voice is ours or someone else's.

Although others may be hardened against recognizing the word of God that comes through us, our empowerment enables us to move ahead, even against resistance, whether it be external or internal. If we accept God's word and power, we are a sign to the Pharaohs of our world that no God exists but the God who is just and merciful.

Reflection and Journal-writing Exercises

1. Two main themes flow throughout this meditation: empowerment and hardening of the heart.
- Reflect first on a situation in which the Pharaoh within you hardened or is hardening your heart.
- Talk with your Pharaoh. Imagine that you are sitting before him as his counselor, trying to convince him to listen to God's voice. Write out the conversation.

2. Turn to the Moses within you who has been energized and empowered.
- Recall some moments when you seemed to have a power, an authority, a moral rightness that was not ordinary for you. Recall all the details: who was there, what was done, the outcome, and so on. How did you feel afterward?
- Do you believe that when God commissions you, you will receive the necessary power to do as you are commanded?

3. Compose a prayer that both asks God's forgiveness for a time when you hardened your heart and praises God for a time when you were energized and empowered with divine strength. Refer to specific rather than general moments in your life.

Memory Verse

Take this verse with you in your heart and on your lips:

Thy hands have made and fashioned me. . . .

(Ps. 119:73)

CHET: *The letter* chet *stands for both the He-brew word for sin and the Hebrew word for life. A sinner can break the habit of sin through repentance, which brings life.*

Increasing Resistance

God relentlessly seeks to deliver humankind from the power of evil, even using the destructive forces in nature to bring about freedom.

Each plague, meant to convince Pharaoh of God's power and love, causes Pharaoh to further harden his heart against the persistent God who is following ever more closely at his heels. As a result of the plagues, Pharaoh finally gives in to God, and the Israelites are free to leave and to worship the one true God.

As you read about the effects of the plagues on Pharaoh, reflect on the effect of trials and misfortunes in your own life. Do you regard trials as invitations to know yourself and your God more intimately, or do they prompt you to retreat in bitterness or apathetic resignation?

Exodus 7:20—11:10

> Moses and Aaron did as the LORD commanded; in the sight of Pharaoh and in the sight of his servants, he lifted up the rod and struck the water that was in the Nile, and all the water that was in the Nile turned to blood. . . . Pharaoh turned and went into his house, and he did not lay even this to heart. . . .

. . . So Aaron stretched out his hand over the waters of Egypt; and the frogs came up and covered the land of Egypt. . . .

. . . But . . . Pharaoh . . . hardened his heart, and would not listen to them; as the LORD had said. . . .

. . . Aaron stretched out his hand with his rod, and struck the dust of the earth, and there came gnats on man and beast; all the dust of the earth became gnats throughout all the land of Egypt. . . . But Pharaoh's heart was hardened, and he would not listen to them; as the LORD had said.

. . . There came great swarms of flies into the house of Pharaoh and into his servants' houses, and in all the land of Egypt the land was ruined by reason of the flies.

. . . But Pharaoh hardened his heart this time also, and did not let the people go.

. . . And on the morrow the LORD did this thing; all the cattle of the Egyptians died. . . . But the heart of Pharaoh was hardened, and he did not let the people go.

. . . So they took ashes from the kiln, and stood before Pharaoh, and Moses threw them toward heaven, and it became boils breaking out in sores on man and beast. . . . But the LORD hardened the heart of Pharaoh, and he did not listen to them; as the LORD had spoken to Moses. . . .

. . . Then Moses stretched forth his rod toward heaven; and the LORD sent thunder and hail, and fire ran down to the earth. . . . The hail struck down everything that was in the field. . . .

. . . So the heart of Pharaoh was hardened, and he did not let the people of Israel go; as the LORD had spoken through Moses. . . .

. . . And the locusts came up over all the land of Egypt. . . . They covered the face of the whole land, . . . they ate all the plants in the land. . . . But the LORD hardened Pharaoh's heart, and he did not let the children of Israel go.

. . . So Moses stretched out his hand toward heaven, and there was thick darkness in all the land of Egypt three days. . . . But the LORD hardened Pharaoh's heart, and he would not let them go. . . .

And Moses said, "Thus says the LORD: About midnight I will go forth in the midst of Egypt; and all the first-born in the land of Egypt shall die. . . ."

Moses and Aaron did all these wonders before Pharaoh; and the LORD hardened Pharaoh's heart, and he did not let the people of Israel go out of his land.

Commentary

The above verses have been arranged so that each plague and Pharaoh's reaction to it are evident. According to the biblical writer, the plagues result from Pharaoh's hardening of heart. Before any of the plagues occurred, everything positive had been done to convince Pharaoh to let the Israelites go to worship God. The first step was a simple message brought to him from God through Moses: "Let my people go." Pharaoh's negative response to this request hardened his heart. If Pharaoh was cruel before, he became even crueler now.

The second step was when God prompted Pharaoh to listen to Moses because he was as God (Exod. 7:1). But Pharaoh would have no other gods than himself.

The third step was a manifestation of signs and miracles (Exod. 7:8–13). Pharaoh dismissed these as insignificant because his own magicians could do the same, and the God of Moses seemed no more powerful than Pharaoh and his gods.

Now, the first six plagues, each one worse than the previous one, begin to crack Pharaoh's resistance to the God of Moses. The first, in which the water of the Nile is changed into blood, is dismissed by Pharaoh as a mere nuisance. Because his own magicians are just as powerful in this respect, Pharaoh turns and goes into his house, and he does not take even this to heart.

The second plague, an infestation of frogs, prompts a slight shift in Pharaoh's attitude. Although his magicians can also bring frogs upon the land, they cannot get rid of them. So Pharaoh tells Moses and Aaron to plead with the Lord to remove the frogs and that in return he will let the people go. However, as soon as the prayer is answered, Pharaoh changes his mind. He is not ready to submit to a God greater than his own.

The third plague, gnats, is beyond the power of the magicians. Seeing "'the finger of God,'" they warn Pharaoh that a superior power is at work. Pharaoh cannot allow himself to listen to the magicians, for if he does, he will have to recognize that his own power is threatened.

When a fourth plague, flies, ruins the land, Pharaoh indicates that he is ready to bargain, but even at this point he is trying to deal with God on even terms. He will allow the Israelites to worship God, but only within the land of Egypt. Moses— formerly a hesitant, reluctant man on a mission but now fully God's prophet—refuses to bargain. Unwilling to compromise the will of God, Moses responds to Pharaoh's offer, "'It would not be right to do this.'"

A fifth plague, more terrible than the others, invades the land and causes all the cattle to die. The magicians have already recognized the finger of God, and now God's whole hand, not just a finger, is manifested. Pharaoh, who consistently has hardened his heart and refused to recognize the finger of God, is now unable to recognize God's hand.

The sixth plague, inflammation, affects not only animals but people as well. Pharaoh is now so hardened against giving up his power that he cannot comply with Moses' request. For the first time in the account of the plagues, the narrative states that God, the Divine Self, "hardened the heart of Pharaoh." After all, because we are made in God's image, we are free to love God or resist God. Thus when Pharaoh hardens his heart, God can be said to cause the hardening because it is the result of the freedom of choice granted to humans from the dawn of Creation. To the writers of Exodus, God, by allowing Pharaoh to resist, hardens Pharaoh's heart. At no time is Pharaoh excused for his decisions, and the human power for evil joins with the forces of destruction in nature to wreak havoc in the land. Yet

God is still fully in charge of all of this, using it to bring freedom to the Israelites.

Exod. 9:13—11:10 is an account of the seventh, eighth, and ninth plagues of hail and thunder, of locusts, and of darkness, respectively. It also includes the announcement of the final plague, the death of the firstborn sons. After this announcement, the story pauses for the introduction of the Passover theme; then it continues to tell of the occurrence of the tenth plague and the subsequent liberation of the Israelites.

Beginning with the seventh plague, the descriptions become more detailed, an indication that a sickness unto death is sweeping the country. The hailstones are so large that animals and people are killed by their impact, grass is flattened, and trees are shattered. Pharaoh calls Moses and Aaron to him and confesses for the first time, "'I have sinned this time; the LORD is in the right, and I and my people are in the wrong. Entreat the LORD . . . [and] I will let you go. . . .'"

The plagues, though destructive, are revealing a power above all human power and above that of all the gods imaged by humans. The God of Moses is not just another God but the Creator of heaven and earth, who existed before the world was created and who will continue to exist when the world comes to its end. Yet despite this revelation of God to Pharaoh, he is not delivered. Pharaoh has neither love nor fear of God. He regards God as a combatant who has the upper hand for the present. A true, freeing relationship between this human creature and the Creator is not possible.

Convinced that Pharaoh has no fear of God, Moses begs God to remove the plague of hail so that Pharaoh might be moved by God's mercy if not by God's power. But no sooner does the hail cease falling than Pharaoh and his courtiers revert to their guilty ways. Again Pharaoh is warned to let the people go lest locusts be allowed to devour the remaining greenery on the earth. Pharaoh's courtiers, who previously sided with him, now accost him, "How long shall this one be a snare to us? Let the people go to worship the Lord their God! Are you not aware that Egypt is ruined?" But Pharaoh continues to resist. The locusts come in such thick masses that the land is darkened by their number. Anything that remains after the hailstorm is devoured by these insects. Nothing green is left, of tree or of grass of the fields, in all the land of Egypt.

Pharaoh hurriedly summons Moses and Aaron, pleads guilty, and makes the same promises, only to retract them when the plague is lifted. This time a darkness so thick that it can be felt descends upon the land. This darkness is not merely the absence of light that can be dispelled by lighting a fire; it is indicative of the darkness that has invaded the soul and mind of Pharaoh. Pharaoh has hardened his heart to the revelations of God and to the cry of his own people, and because of his unwillingness to recognize God as the Lord, the land has become desolate and the people are in anguish.

Reflection and Journal-writing Exercises

According to the Exodus story, redemption is "'that you may know that there is no one like the LORD our God.'" Knowledge and worship of God are the highest goals of human life, and the most rewarding.

Egyptian Pharaohs considered themselves gods and were treated as such by their subjects. So in the Exodus story, Pharaoh resists any suggestion that he is a mortal subject to a God whose representative is a lowly Hebrew.

But are we not subject to the same temptation as Pharaoh is? Is it not all too common for us to want to control life, to think and act as if we determine our destiny? We resist God's will; we harden our heart to the word of God, the cries of poor people, the sight of hungry and naked people. In the process we become enslaved by our own need to control and to be secure.

1. One of the great values of illness and adversity is that they shock us. We realize in startling ways that we are not God. Now would be a good time in our journey to appreciate our plagues and trials.
- Relax. Recall that the all-knowing and faithful God is with you now in this moment, in this place.

- Bring to mind and to heart your last bout of illness or a recent time of anguish and trial for you. Spend some time, eyes closed, recalling every aspect of your illness or trial: who was there, what happened, how you felt, and so on. Replay the whole episode. When you are finished, continue to the next step of the meditation.
- Meditate on the effects that this illness or trial had on you. Did you change any behaviors because of it? Do you see life differently in any way? Did it touch you for a while but not really have any long-range effect? Ponder these questions.
- Spend some time dialoguing with God. Ask God what you were supposed to learn from your illness or trial. If you were like Pharaoh and hardened your heart, discuss this with God and make peace.

2. Write out what the Lord has told you in this meditation. Record one change that you want to make in your life as a response to God's faithful love.

Memory Verse

Take this verse with you in your heart and on your lips:

> Though the cords of the wicked ensnare me,
>   I do not forget thy law.
>
> (Ps. 119:61)

KOF: *The vertical line of* kof *is the person call-ing* Qadhosh, *or "Holy, Holy, Holy." The curved line bending downward is the sign of God's all-encompassing love and protection.*

Deliverance

After the announcement of the tenth plague, but before its oc-currence, God commands the people of Israel to celebrate the Passover ritual. This feast is to be an annual celebration to com-memorate their deliverance. It is a ritual of remembering and worshiping. The performance of this ritual is not left to the whims and vacillations of the celebrators. Rather, God pre-scribes details on how to commemorate and relive the experi-ence. By remembering what God has done for them in the Passover and by reenacting the deliverance, the people are as-sured of maintaining the freedom and faith to continue their journey.

Exodus 12:1–32

> The LORD said to Moses and Aaron in the land of Egypt, "This month shall be for you the beginning of months; it shall be the first month of the year for you. Tell all the con-gregation of Israel that on the tenth day of this month they shall take every [one] a lamb according to their [ancestors'] houses, a lamb for a household; and if the household is too small for a lamb, then [they and their] neighbor next to [their] house shall take according to the number of persons;

according to what each can eat you shall make your count for the lamb. Your lamb shall be without blemish . . . ; you shall take it from the sheep or from the goats; and you shall keep it until the fourteenth day of this month, when the whole assembly of the congregation of Israel shall kill their lambs in the evening. Then they shall take some of the blood, and put it on the two doorposts and the lintel of the houses in which they eat them. They shall eat the flesh that night, roasted; with unleavened bread and bitter herbs they shall eat it. . . . In this manner you shall eat it: your loins girded, your sandals on your feet, and your staff in your hand; and you shall eat it in haste. It is the LORD's passover.". . .

Then the people of Israel went and did so; as the LORD had commanded Moses and Aaron, so they did.

At midnight the LORD smote all the first-born in the land of Egypt, from the first-born of Pharaoh who sat on his throne to the first-born of the captive who was in the dungeon, and all the first-born of the cattle. And Pharaoh rose up in the night, he, and all his servants, and all the Egyptians; and there was a great cry in Egypt, for there was not a house where one was not dead. And he summoned Moses and Aaron by night, and said, "Rise up, go forth from among my people, both you and the people of Israel; and go, serve the LORD, as you have said. Take your flocks and your herds, as you have said, and be gone; and bless me also!"

Commentary

The central purpose of the Passover celebration is for the Israelites to recall the great act of deliverance on the part of the Lord their God and to gratefully worship. It is to be the national celebration of their passage from slavery to their becoming a people. God orders the Passover ritual to be celebrated even before Pharaoh submits and lets the people of Israel go. Even before the actual events of the passage come to pass, God shows the Israelites that God will be with them.

Like all festivals, Passover incorporates meaningful symbols. The Passover celebration is both a family and a community celebration. Its preparation and celebration fall not upon any one sector of the community but upon the whole people. All persons, together as a community, and each one individually are to remember that they were saved and delivered both as a people and as unique individuals. This ritual reenactment and reliving of the original experience of deliverance from bondage will safeguard freedom and worship of God as cherished and enduring values.

The blood of a lamb is to be put on the two doorposts and the lintel of each house. Blood stands for one's life, which is offered willingly for the love of God and neighbor. When the angel of death passes and sees this sign of dedication and commitment to God, the lives of those within the household are spared. True liberation demands sacrifice.

Other symbols are the hurry with which the meal is to be eaten, the sandals on the feet, the staff in hand—all indicating readiness for the passage and the idea that deliverance is not the end of the journey but the beginning. The passage of deliverance from Pharaoh is only the start of the journey to becoming a people and to reaching the Promised Land.

Eating unleavened bread symbolizes that an old and usual way of life is over and a new way of life is to begin.

When Passover is celebrated, these rituals remind us, as they reminded Moses and the Israelites, that even though the passage to freedom and the journey to new life that follow might be difficult, God is a faithful God who keeps the promise to deliver people from bondage and to lead them to their destiny as a people of God.

To further add to the hope and joy of Passover, no work is to be done on the first and seventh days of the festival. The ability to stop work is, in itself, a sign of liberation. In God's plan there is time to play.

Should the annual celebration of Passover not be sufficient for the people to remember their deliverance, a further stipulation is given to the community: "'It shall be as a mark on your hand or frontlets between your eyes; for by a strong hand the LORD brought us out of Egypt'" (Exod. 13:16). Scriptural passages written on pieces of parchment are put into small boxes attached to the forehead and arm with leather bands. (Some Jewish men, and occasionally women, wore these boxes every time they went out in public. In time, the practice was restricted to certain hours and occasions.) Ritual celebration with religious symbolism helps keep the Israelites in touch with their God as they continue their journey to the Promised Land.

Initial freedom is only a beginning in the spiritual journey. The human spirit, like the community of Israel, although free to go forth, is still a tribal rabble, an unorganized collection of feelings, thoughts, and actions. It needs to grow in unity and wholeness.

The sanctifying, integrating power of the Lord is still to come. It will come in the hungers and thirsts of the desert, in the conflicts and rivalries within the households, and in the deceptions and temptations of illusions and mirages. God's power will be seen in the cloud and in the pillar of fire and will work through the manna, the water from the rock, and the faithful ones.

Rites and symbols of passage are important for remembering times when God delivered us. During new passages and the tough times in the journey that follows, reminders of previous passages and journeys will sustain and encourage you. God is present; God remains faithful to you amidst community, in trials and sacrifices, and in the journey you are about to take in the next segment of your exodus.

Reflection and Journal-writing Exercises

1. Reread the scriptural passage slowly, aloud or in a whisper. Stay with the words or phrases that especially catch your attention.
- Write down three or four of these phrases.
- Repeat the phrases slowly to yourself. One of the phrases will speak to you more than the others do. Stay with this phrase,

absorbing its message the way the thirsty earth receives the rain. Become aware of the feelings and desires that are awakened within you.

- In your journal, describe why this phrase is especially significant for you.

2. Recall several deliverance times in your life, times when you were freed spiritually and physically to move ahead. Did you, or do you now, recognize God in these times?

3. Do you have personal rituals or memorabilia to help you remember these passage times? What are they? If you have personal rituals, let images of these rituals form in your memory; act out these rituals. If you have memorabilia, find them, if possible, and hold them in your hands. Let them evoke memories and feelings of the passages they symbolize. Is your spirit free now, or is it in need of new deliverance?

4. In your journal, write your reflections on this meditation.

Memory Verse

Take this verse with you in your heart and on your lips:

With my whole heart I cry; answer me, O LORD!

(Ps. 119:145)

DALET: *The letter* dalet *stands for "judge" (dayan). God is both a God who judges and a God of mercy. Justice and mercy complement each other. The just God judges each person according to deeds done. The merciful God is always ready to open the door of mercy to the repentant sinner.*

Into the Desert

In the Book of Exodus, the desert is the land between Mitzraim, the land of bondage, and Sinai, the mountain of God. The desert is the two-edged instrument with which the Divine Physician cuts away and heals the evils that have been inflicted through slavery. The Israelites learn that the way of purgation is long and slow (meditation 11). They travel to Sinai, not along the well-traveled trade route of the caravans but through a vast wilderness with no roads and no signs of civilization. As they move deeper into this wilderness (meditations 12 and 13), shedding more and more of the trappings of civilization and the mentality of an enslaved people, their minds are purified, their hearts warmed, their wills strengthened. Their daily nourishment is the will of God and manna from heaven. In meditation 14, they finally arrive at a juncture, where they are attacked by the Amalekites, a fierce clan of desert warriors. With nothing more to lose, nothing more to fear except the loss of life itself, they fight and win. A new kind of talk is heard among the leaders of the Israelites and throughout their camps (meditation 15): "Have you heard all that God has done for us? God is our strength and our song, our protector, our savior. You, O Holy One, shall reign forever."

The stages of the spiritual journey have often been described as purgation, illumination, and union. These periods do not necessarily follow in sequential order but often occur together, with one of them predominating. The desert experience is primarily that of purgation. It includes the dark night of the senses and the soul and often is the experience of death. Yet the time in the desert is also a time of illumination and union. The long periods of dryness and isolation have moments of jubilation and victory over personal demons, nourishment with bread from heaven, and assurances that this bread will not depart as long as the sojourn in the desert lasts.

As you make this part of the journey with the Israelites, pray that because your deepest will is to be faithful and to persevere, God will take you at your word and ensure your fidelity throughout all your dark nights:

O God, Creator of heaven and earth, direct my mind and body throughout this day and make me holy. Keep me faithful to your law in thought, word, and deed. Be my helper now and always; free me from sin and bring all peoples to salvation in your Kingdom, where you live and reign forever and ever. Amen.

SHIN: Shin *represents two names of God:* El Shaddai, *"the All-powerful One," and* Shalom, *or "Peace." After the Israelites escape Pharaoh's armies, they sing triumphantly,*
> *"Who is like thee, O LORD, among the gods?*
>
> · · · · · · · · · ·
>
> *. . . terrible in glorious deeds, doing wonders?"*
>
> (Exod. 15:11)

Beginning of the Journey

As the Israelites set out on their journey, they discover that God is not leading them by the short, well-traveled route but rather by a long, roundabout, unused one. Still elated with their triumph over Pharaoh and visibly guided by God's hovering presence, they are compliant and obedient to divine guidance. However, once they realize that Pharaoh has changed his mind and is pursuing them, their newly won confidence changes to panic and fear, causing them to forget all that God has done for them. Reassured by Moses' comforting words and miraculously delivered by the power of God, they cross safely through the waters of the Red Sea and, seeing their enemy destroyed behind them, burst into the triumphant Song of the Sea.

Although many have gone on the spiritual journey, the path each person must travel is unknown and often circuitous. Like the road for the Israelites, our path will take us into a wilderness through which we must be led. Sometimes God is clearly present and at other times apparently absent. We too will have our faith tested, our memory of God's deeds questioned, and our determination to seek and worship God threatened by Pharaoh's pursuing army. Then, prevailing over these dark forces, our heart will burst into a song of triumph.

Ask the Lord to help you set your face toward the future, strong in faith and determination despite the opposing forces you will encounter.

Exodus 13:17—14:29

When Pharaoh let the people go, God did not lead them by way of the land of the Philistines, although that was near; for God said, "Lest the people repent when they see war, and return to Egypt." But God led the people round by the way of the wilderness toward the Red Sea. . . . And the LORD went before them by day in a pillar of cloud to lead them along the way, and by night in a pillar of fire to give them light, that they might travel by day and by night. . . .

When the king of Egypt was told that the people had fled, the mind of Pharaoh and his servants was changed toward [Israel]. . . . The Egyptians pursued them, all Pharaoh's horses and chariots and his horsemen and his army, and overtook them encamped at the sea. . . .

When Pharaoh drew near, the people of Israel lifted up their eyes, and behold, the Egyptians were marching after them; and they were in great fear. And the people of Israel cried out to the LORD; and they said to Moses, "Is it because there are no graves in Egypt that you have taken us away to die in the wilderness? What have you done to us, in bringing us out of Egypt? Is not this what we said to you in Egypt, 'Let us alone and let us serve the Egyptians'? For it would have been better for us to serve the Egyptians than to die in the wilderness." And Moses said to the people, "Fear not, stand firm, and see the salvation of the LORD, which [the LORD] will work for you today; for the Egyptians whom you see today, you shall never see again.". . .

Then the LORD said to Moses, "Stretch out your hand over the sea, that the water may come back upon the Egyptians, upon their chariots, and upon their horsemen.". . . The waters returned and covered the chariots and the horsemen and all the host of Pharaoh that had followed them into the sea; not so much as one of them remained. But the people of Israel walked on dry ground through the sea, the waters being a wall to them on their right hand and on their left.

Commentary

Freed from Egypt, the Israelites do not sit around rejoicing and luxuriating in their freedom; rather, they set out for Sinai and the Promised Land. Freedom for freedom's sake is not a biblical goal. Instead, freedom is a condition for true worship of God, which is the ultimate human goal, leading to holiness and self-fulfillment.

In one sense, the worst may be over, for to start a journey is always difficult. In another sense, the real difficulties are just beginning. New foes, both internal and external, lurk along the way. Moses and the people soon discover that they are not going by way of the Philistines, the shortest and most familiar way, but by a route they do not know. God, knowing that the people still possess a slave mentality and are unclear about their destiny, announces the reason for the change: "'Lest the people repent when they see war, and return to Egypt.'" God, not Moses or the people, chooses the way and goes before them in a pillar of cloud by day and in a pillar of fire by night. Visibly surrounded and protected by the Divine Presence, the hearts of the people are pliant and joyful. When God tells the Israelites to turn back from the direction in which they are headed, they do so with no questions or hesitation. Obedience is easy when all is going well.

A first big step in the spiritual journey often brings the sweetness of God's presence. Because God is so tangibly present, obedience is easy, and we make all sorts of rash promises and resolutions. Ignorance is bliss—but not for long.

Regretting that Moses has won and left him without his slave work force, Pharaoh tries to overtake the Israelites. His pride and ambition finally drive him to his death. If only he had let the Israelites be free, he would have saved his life. But he could not do this, so he drowns in the waters of his possessiveness.

The sight of Pharaoh's approaching army shakes the Israelites out of their newfound security and confidence. They forget all that God has done for them and cry out against Moses and God. Such a change of heart is not uncommon for the newly converted or overly confident person. At the first crisis, doubt enters and one asks, Why did I ever start out? Why didn't I stay where I was?

Here, the Israelites' journey corresponds to the internal struggle among the different aspects of one's personality. In a crisis, the beaten-down elements of the personality react according to their timeworn grooves, often with blame, self-pity, and apathy. On the other hand, the believing elements—the Moses, the Aaron, and the Miriam—respond with faith, hope, and courage: "'Fear not, stand firm, and see the salvation of the LORD, which [the LORD] will work for you today.'"

When people experience an event with faith, as an event of God, song is a natural response. The Israelites, seeing their miraculous redemption from the pursuing army of Pharaoh, break into song (Exod. 15:1–21), of which a paraphrase follows:

> I will sing to you, O LORD, for you are gloriously
> > triumphant;
> > horse and rider you have cast into the sea.
> You are my strength and my song;
> > you are my savior.
> My God, I praise you;
> > God of my ancestors, I extol you.
> You are my protector;
> > great is your name!

Pharaoh's chariots and army you hurled into the sea.
At a breath of your anger the waters piled up,
    the flowing waters stood like a mound,
    the flood waters congealed in the midst of the sea.
The enemy boasted, "I will pursue and overtake them,
    I will divide the spoils and have my fill of them,
    I will draw my sword; my hand shall despoil them!"
When your wind blew, the sea covered them;
    like lead they sank in the mighty waters.
    Who is like you among the gods?
    Who is like to you, magnificent in holiness?
O terrible in renown, worker of wonders,
    when you stretched out your right hand,
    the earth swallowed them!

In your faithful love you led the people you redeemed;
    In your strength you guided them to your holy
        dwelling.
And you brought them in and planted them on the
    mountain of your abode—
    the place where you made your sanctuary, O LORD,
    the sanctuary that your hands established.
You, O LORD, shall reign forever.

The song is a triumphant exclamation. It has the power to reinstill hope and trust in the whole community. Israel knows that it has been saved by the power of God. When salvation was offered to Pharaoh, he refused it, for he would have had to admit that he was not God, that he was not in control, that Another was more powerful than he was. Pharaoh would not admit that he was finite.

To admit that we are finite is to accept being vulnerable and, one day, having to die. To deny that we are finite is to avoid looking at our vulnerability and mortality. It means clothing the self in a thick armor of defense: wealth, property, personal titles, and so on. These give us the false hope of being attached to something stronger and more endurable than the naked self. Letting go of any of these supports is frightening. What would happen to a person stripped of all support? The temptation is to never let go and never find out.

Painful as it may be, we have no alternative in the journey to God but to let go of all false supports. T. S. Eliot wrote,

> In order to arrive at what you are not
> You must go through the way in which you are not.
>   ("East Coker," *Four Quartets*, p. 29)

The Gospel counsels, "'. . . Unless a grain of wheat falls into the earth and dies, it remains alone; but if it dies, it bears much fruit'" (John 12:24).

Reflection and Journal-writing Exercises

This meditation describes the ebb and flow of our relationship with God. Knowing that God is leading, recognizing the surrounding and protecting Divine Presence, and bursting into melody in the Song of the Sea are all examples of the flow and expansiveness of our religious emotions. Flow and expansiveness, however, alternate with ebb and contraction. The ebb can be seen in the fear that invades the hearts of the Israelites at the sight of Pharaoh's army and in the panic that overtakes them at the threat of losing their freedom.

The ebb and flow experienced by the Israelites is not uncommon in the spiritual life of a person. At one moment, a person can be filled with delight in God and at another moment be empty and alone. Mystics call the intense times of ebb in spiritual life "the dark night of the soul." The clarity of the mind's judgment fades and is replaced by a maze of doubt and uncertainty. This confusion and obscurity is the result not of an absence of God but of the human person's incapacity to fully receive the overwhelming light and love that pours forth from God.

1. Recall one time when you experienced the ebb and flow of God's presence in your life.
- What factors caused the ebb and flow?
- Did the ebb and flow follow the same pattern as it did for the Israelites: joy, doubt, fear, jubilation?

2. Recall a second experience.
- What factors caused the ebb and flow?
- Did the ebb and flow follow the same pattern as it did for the Israelites: joy, doubt, fear, jubilation?

3. The words of the Israelites' song, "You are my savior. My God, I praise you," when recited with faith, give power to surrender. This part of the second verse of the song has been translated variously from Hebrew using the words *praise, glorify,* and *enshrine.* With the translation *enshrine,* it reads, "You are my savior, my God whom I enshrine." Try praying this sentence by putting an accent on different words. First put the accent on *my.* Although God is the God of my ancestors, God will only be "my" God when I personally find God. Then put the accent on *enshrine.* I "enshrine" God when I receive and respond to the Divine within my own being. The goal of life is to become an ever more fit dwelling place for the Lord, a temple for the Holy of Holies.

4. Compose a prayer along the lines of the Song of the Sea that includes exaltation of God's saving power, a description of an event in which you experienced God's saving power, and adoration and praise for the wonders of God.

5. Write in your journal any insights this meditation has given you.

Memory Verse

Take this verse with you in your heart and on your lips:

> Princes persecute me without cause,
>   but my heart stands in awe of thy words.

(Ps. 119:161)

RESH: Resh *stands for both* resha, *"wicked-ness," and* rachamim, *"mercy." It is symbolic of the choice between holiness and sin and also of reconciliation. When* resh, *as a sinner, repents,* resh, *as mercy, always forgives.*

Entering the Wilderness

The wilderness is the last place one would expect a liberated people to go. Yet the Israelites leave the known for the unknown, a stable existence for an unstable one, a fixed dwelling place for a place of no abode. Why? The answer defies all human logic.

The Israelites go into the wilderness because that is where God leads them. They do not ask how long they will have to stay there or whether they will ever get out again. At this point, they have little sense of the divine intimacy to which they are being called and cannot imagine what it is like to be a people of God. Neither do they know of the hardships ahead or of their own stubbornness, rebellion, and even idolatry. All the Israelites know is that they must obey the mysterious call and go by a route no one else has traveled before.

As you begin this meditation, pause and ask yourself if you are ready to continue the journey. Can you go on regardless of the obstacles you might meet? Fidelity to prayer and God's graciousness to you are strong guarantees that you will be able to continue following your call.

Exodus 15:22–27

Then Moses led Israel onward from the Red Sea, and they went into the wilderness of Shur; they went three days in the wilderness and found no water. When they came to Marah, they could not drink the water of Marah because it was bitter; therefore it was named Marah. And the people murmured against Moses, saying, "What shall we drink?" And he cried to the LORD; and the LORD showed him a tree, and he threw it into the water, and the water became sweet.

There the LORD made for them a statute and an ordinance and there [the LORD] proved them, saying, "If you will diligently hearken to [my] voice, . . . and do that which is right in [my] eyes, and give heed to [my] commandments and keep all [my] statutes, I will put none of the diseases upon you which I put upon the Egyptians; for I am the LORD, your healer."

Then they came to Elim, where there were twelve springs of water and seventy palm trees; and they encamped there by the water.

Commentary

For three days the Israelites travel in the wilderness but find no water. A person journeying in the desert of the Sinai peninsula, with its hot, relentless sun, might panic at the very thought of no water, but the Israelites travel for days with no water in sight. Imagine what it might be like to lead tribes of people, including the elderly and the young, through this territory with no water to give them! Despite how elated the Israelites were at the miracles wrought for them at the Red Sea, now they are worried and apprehensive. They can see nothing but dry, trackless wasteland ahead of them.

Every ounce of their faith is tested. Where is God now? Did they really meet this God, or was it all an illusion?

When they finally arrive at Marah, they find water but cannot drink it. Not only is the water bitter, but their own souls are filled with bitterness and disappointment. Moses cries out to God, and God hears him. The Lord shows Moses a piece of wood that will sweeten the water. The spirits of those who drink it will be lifted.

On the spiritual journey, Marah and Shur stand for periods of trial. *Marah* means "bitterness," the bitterness that comes from frustrated goodwill and the feeling of being betrayed by God. The wilderness of Shur represents the emptiness that is experienced when the trappings of the outside world are left behind. To face one's self in poverty and nakedness is frightening and often prompts self-doubt. Has a mistake been made? Would it have been better to remain a submissive, law-abiding slave? When these doubts and questions arise, another voice, the Moses voice, goes to God for help. God hears the cry of anguish, and the pilgrim finds a way to survive and continue the journey.

At Marah, God gives the people a fixed rule—not a rule to be kept once but a rule that will endure. When followed, this self-discipline maintains a diligent listening to God's word and a faithful following of that word.

Without self-discipline, we never get far on the spiritual journey. Energies, which are easily dissipated, need to be harnessed and recharged for the long trek ahead.

The springs of Elim are a sign of the abundant nourishment available to those who accept God's statutes as a rule of life. Moses and the Israelites find not only one spring but twelve, not one tree but seventy. The twelve springs ensure that enough water flows for all of the Twelve Tribes of Israel. They can also be seen as signs that there will always be enough spiritual nourishment for all humans, regardless of race or calling. Further, the twelve springs can signify that all the different aspects of one's personality are to be nurtured to full growth.

The seventy trees represent the seventy elders who helped Moses lead the people in the desert. They can also represent those aspects of one's psyche that are developed enough to help lead the rest of the self on the inner journey to wholeness.

For those who listen and hear, God's providence in the wilderness is abundant and life-giving.

Reflection and Journal-writing Exercises

The way of the wilderness is the way to a renewed self. In the wilderness, one is divested of false pride and ambition.

1. Sit quietly before God and recall a wilderness period in your life.
- What fears did you experience? What caused them? Were there signs of God's presence? What were they?
- Through this wilderness experience, what aspects of your personality were called to full growth?
- What were your seventy elders—those aspects of your character that gave you strength?
- Did God's provident care come to you? How?

2. Repeat the following sentence over and over, emphasizing a different word each time: Speak, Lord, your servant is listening.

3. Write in your journal what you heard and felt as you relived the wilderness experience in your memory. Compare it with the Israelites' experience in the wilderness.
- Would any of your pain have been avoided through fidelity to a rule of life, a life-giving discipline?
- Do you have a rule of life now?

Memory Verse

Take this verse with you in your heart and on your lips:

Many are my persecutors and my adversaries,
but I do not swerve from thy testimonies.

(Ps. 119:157)

AYIN: *This letter and the Hebrew word for* eye *have the same sound, which is* ayin. *The number ten (*aseret*) in the phrase* Ten Commandments *begins with* ayin, *as does* Tree of Life *(*ets ha-chayin*). Those who keep God's commandments see and eat the fruits of the Tree of Life.*

Deeper into the Wilderness

Entering more deeply into the wilderness is symbolic of being drawn more deeply into the mystery of God's presence and self-disclosure. Such nearness to God makes obedience crucial and confidence and trust in God imperative. Yet there are feelings both of deep attachment to God and of unreasonable resistance to surrender to God's will. The Sabbath, a time for work stoppage and rest, is given as a gift to the traveler who is moving ever nearer to the mountain of God.

Travel with the Israelites as they go deeper into the wilderness. Repent with them for doubts and lack of faith. Join them in gathering and eating the bread from heaven. Be drawn with them to the blazing glory of God.

Exodus 16:1–35

They set out from Elim, and all the congregation of the people of Israel came to the wilderness of Sin, which is between Elim and Sinai, on the fifteenth day of the second month after they had departed from the land of Egypt. And the whole congregation of the people of Israel murmured against Moses and Aaron in the wilderness. . . .

Then the LORD said to Moses, "Behold, I will rain bread from heaven for you; and the people shall go out and gather a day's portion every day, that I may prove them, whether they will walk in my law or not. On the sixth day, when they prepare what they bring in, it will be twice as much as they gather daily.". . .

. . . And the people of Israel did so; they gathered, some more, some less. But when they measured it with an omer, [they] that gathered much had nothing over, and [they] that gathered little had no lack; each gathered according to what [they] could eat. And Moses said to them, "Let no [one] leave any of it till the morning." But they did not listen to Moses; some left part of it till the morning, and it bred worms and became foul; and Moses was angry with them. . . .

. . . [Moses] said to them, "This is what the LORD has commanded: 'Tomorrow is a day of solemn rest, a holy sabbath to the LORD; bake what you will bake and boil what you will boil, and all that is left over lay by to be kept till the morning.'" So they laid it by till the morning, as Moses bade them; and it did not become foul, and there were no worms in it. . . . On the seventh day some of the people went out to gather, and they found none. And the LORD said to Moses, "How long do you refuse to keep my commandments and my laws?". . .

. . . And the people of Israel ate the manna forty years, till they came to a habitable land; they ate the manna, till they came to the border of the land of Canaan.

Commentary

No sooner have the people left the springs of Elim than they encounter their first difficulties and all the old complaints and doubts reappear. "'Would that we had died by the hand of the

LORD in the land of Egypt, when we sat by the fleshpots and ate bread to the full.'" To the people who are frightened at the thought of dying in the desert, the old slavery and food look good. The more they reflect on "the good old days," the more apprehensive and disgruntled they become. For the first time in the biblical text, we read that the entire congregation is murmuring.

The intensity of doubt and discontent that has taken over the people is shocking when we consider all that God has done for them. Each time the people grumble and disobey, God promises food and rest. Although God seems dismayed at their murmuring, God has no angry punishment for the people. Rather, God promises more food and rest. And the Lord says to Moses, "I hear the murmurings of the Israelites. Tell them this: 'Tonight you shall eat flesh, and in the morning, bread. Then you will know that I am the Lord.'" Even in the acceptance of that food, some of the people, continuing their antagonism, disobey the orders for gathering it.

What is God doing? With immense patience, God is preparing the people for the great encounter at Mount Sinai. Not only is each complaint answered with a promise of food, but the people are given glimpses of God's glory.

Several times in this chapter God's glory is manifested: When the people grumble, Aaron says to them, "By evening you shall know it was the Lord because the Lord has heard your grumblings against the Lord." As Aaron talks to the people, they turn toward the wilderness, and there, in a cloud, appears the presence of the Lord. Likewise, Moses announces to them that when morning arrives and their stomachs are full, they will know that the Lord is God.

By glimpsing the glory of God, their eyes become better able to recognize God's presence with them, and their hearts begin to burn with a desire for more constant and intimate contact with their God.

The Israelites come to know that there is a divine way to do everything, even a divine way to receive a gift. Three rules are attached to receiving the manna. Not all of the people obey these rules.

- *Rule 1:* Gather as much of the manna as each person requires. There is to be no hoarding and no false security. "'Do not lay up for yourselves treasures on earth, where moth and rust consume and where thieves break in and steal, but lay up for yourselves treasures in heaven, where neither moth nor rust consumes and where thieves do not break in and steal. For where your treasure is, there will your heart be also'" (Matt. 6:19–21).

  Response: Although some people have gathered more than they need, when the food is measured, they have the same amount as those who gathered less. In the end, as in death, all are equal.
- *Rule 2:* Save none of the manna until morning. Trust God. "'Look at the birds of the air: they neither sow nor reap nor gather into barns, and yet [God] feeds them. Are you not of more value than they?'" (Matt. 6:26).

  Response: Some keep the manna until the next morning, only to discover that it has become infected with maggots and stinks.
- *Rule 3:* Gather double the amount of manna on the sixth day so that no work will be done on the Sabbath. The Sabbath is holy both unto the Lord and unto the people. To refrain from work is to admit the sovereignty of God and the dependence of the human creature on God.

  Response: Some of the people look for the manna on the seventh day but find none. "Unless the LORD builds the house, those who build it labor in vain" (Ps. 127:1).

All of these rules are connected to trust in God's providence and surrender to the divine will. Trust in God does not mean doing nothing and, like a young bird, expecting God to put food into one's mouth. Rather, it means being like a mother bird going in search of the food that is provided to her each day. Some people follow the divine way; others do not.

Those who disobey are not punished by God; instead they are questioned, "'How long do you refuse to keep my commandments and my laws?'" Although God does not punish the people for their disobedience, they punish themselves by taking the law into their own hands and relying on themselves. They are unable to perceive the gift and see the miracle. On the other hand, those who obey God's commands see the manna as a gift given and are able to rest secure in the providence of God.

Each day for forty years the people live on this manna. Each day they are given their daily portion, except on the sixth day, when they are given a double portion that provides for the Sabbath. More and more, they learn to trust in God. Their lives are dependent solely on God's providence. All comes from God, and all is gift.

Slowly but surely the people are being drawn closer to God and readied for the climactic encounter at Sinai.

Reflection and Journal-writing Exercises

1. Although a food similar to the manna described in the Bible is still found in the Sinai peninsula today, the Israelites did not consider the manna natural food but rather bread from heaven. With this in mind, reflect quietly on the following questions:

• What is the manna—the life-giving, undeserved gift from God—in your life?
• What are its characteristics? What convinces you that this gift is truly from God?
• Is there a discipline involved in receiving the manna?
• What is your response to this discipline?

2. In your journal, write a dialogue with those Israelites who refuse to obey the rules for receiving the manna.
• Ask them why they disobey.
• Talk with them about any problems you have in trusting God's providence or about times when you wanted more than God gave you.

3. Read these words from Psalm 78:

[You] commanded the skies above,
    and opened the doors of heaven;
and [you] rained down upon [me] manna to eat,
    and gave [me] the grain of heaven.
[I] ate of the bread of angels;
    [you] sent [the] food in abundance.

(78:23–25)

Read the passage over and over again, each time substituting the last sentence with words of thanksgiving for a gift that God has sent you. For example, "You sent my friend Sarah to comfort me. For her, thanks and praise."

   4. Close your meditation by composing in your journal a prayer of response to God for the manna received in your life.

Memory Verse

Take this verse with you in your heart and on your lips:

> My eyes fail with watching for thy salvation,
>   and for the fulfillment of thy righteous promise.
> (Ps. 119:123)

SAMECH: Samech, *a closed round letter, is a symbol of support and protection. It stands for* sukah, *which means "tent" or "the dwelling place of God," and* Sinai, *the holy mountain of encounter.*

Fighting the First Battle

The Israelites enter a new phase of their life as they meet the Amalekites. A passive, enslaved people become vigorous; an apathetic people, energized. When the Amalekites attack, the Israelites fight back. They are ready to go to battle so that their journey might continue.

At this point in the journey, they have no halfhearted resistance to the demons that pursue them. A new kind of determination is evident. Committed, assured, and determined to follow their God, the Israelites are ready to die in battle rather than let their enemy stop them from their journey.

Exodus 17:1–15

All the congregation of the people of Israel moved on from the wilderness of Sin by stages, according to the commandment of the LORD, and camped at Rephidim; but there was no water for the people to drink. Therefore the people found fault with Moses, and said, "Give us water to drink." And Moses said to them, "Why do you find fault with me? Why do you put the LORD to the proof?" But the people thirsted there for water, and the people murmured against Moses, and said, "Why did you bring us up out of Egypt, to kill us and our children and our cattle with thirst?" So Moses cried to the LORD, "What shall I do with this people? They are almost ready to stone me." And the LORD said to Moses, "Pass on before the people, taking with you some of the elders of Israel; and take in your hand the rod with which you struck the Nile, and go. Behold, I will stand before you there on the rock at Horeb; and you shall strike the rock, and water shall come out of it, that the people may drink." And Moses did so, in the sight of the elders of Israel. And he called the name of the place Massah and Meribah, because of the faultfinding of the children of Israel, and because they put the LORD to the proof by saying, "Is the LORD among us or not?"

Then came Amalek and fought with Israel at Rephidim. And Moses said to Joshua, "Choose for us men, and go out, fight with Amalek; tomorrow I will stand on the top of the hill with the rod of God in my hand." So Joshua did as Moses told him, and fought with Amalek; and Moses, Aaron, and Hur went up to the top of the hill. Whenever Moses held up his hand, Israel prevailed; and whenever he lowered his hand, Amalek prevailed. But Moses' hands grew weary; so they took a stone and put it under him, and he sat upon it, and Aaron and Hur held up his hands, one on one side, and the other on the other side; so his hands were steady until the going down of the sun. And Joshua mowed down Amalek and his people with the edge of the sword.

. . . And Moses built an altar and called the name of it, The LORD is my banner, saying, "A hand upon the banner of the LORD! . . ."

Commentary

Amalek attacks the Israelites at a place called Rephidim. The immediate cause of the attack seems to be the Israelites' doubt: "'Is the LORD among us or not?'"

For the Israelites, God is like a father who goes on a journey with his son mounted on his shoulders. As the father walks, the son keeps asking for things he sees along the way, and the father gives them to him. After being on the journey for a while, the son, distracted by all the things along the way, loses sight of the fact that he is being carried by his father. They meet a man, and the boy asks the man if he has seen his father. At this, the father puts his son down on the ground. Suddenly a dog comes and bites the boy. Screaming in pain and fear, the boy again recognizes his father and runs to him for protection. Similarly, God has carried the people of Israel and protected them with the Divine Presence—a cloud by day and a pillar of fire by night, which block the path of any lurking enemies. After a time, though, the people of Israel lose sight of God's presence among them. The Amalekites, seeing that they are "alone," attack. The people cry out for help and, once again, return to God.

What causes the people to ask a question like "'Is the LORD among us or not?'" The people have been complaining about the lack of water when suddenly a miraculous event takes place, in which a rock, struck by Moses with his rod, gushes forth life-giving waters. When this event takes place, the Lord stands on the rock before them: "'Behold, I will stand before you there on the rock at Horeb; and you shall strike the rock, and water shall come out of it, that the people may drink.'" Why, then, do the people not see the Lord? Why does the biblical text say that they put the Lord to the test?

First we need to ask the reason for the people's thirst. *Rephidim* means "support and refreshment"; in such a place, the people should not be thirsty. Perhaps while everything was going so well here, they ignored God's rule of life and forgot God.

The word *ignore* means "to turn away." Keeping in touch with God's word is like drawing water from a well; it quenches the deep thirst of the soul. When God's word is ignored, the insatiable thirst for ultimate security cannot be quenched despite the fact that all the necessities of life are present. "Therefore the people found fault with Moses, and said, 'Give us water to drink.'" When God does give them water to drink, they remain unaware of the Divine Presence. Not only does ignoring God's word make the people thirsty, but their turning away prevents them from seeing God, who is standing before them on the rock. To lead them back to the Divine Self, God allows them to experience their human vulnerability.

The Amalekites attack when they see that the people are unprotected. However, because of Israel's faithful members, the Israelites win the battle and return to God. From Rephidim onward there is no mention of a lack of water.

Despite their infidelity and negligence, most of the people have grown in their trust of God. When the Israelites prepare to do battle with the Amalekites, Moses says, "'Choose for us men, and go out, fight. . . .'" There is no hesitation, no delay, in deciding whether to fight the enemy. The word *men,* which is used here, refers not merely to the males but to the mighty ones, those who fear God and merit God's blessings by their righteous living.

While these men fight below, Moses, Aaron, and Hur (Miriam's son) pray on the hilltop. According to tradition, they are not only praying but also fasting. Prayer coupled with fasting is a powerful weapon against the enemy. As Moses prays, he raises his hands heavenward. When he is too weary to hold them up any longer, Aaron and Hur, one on each side of him, hold up his hands. The silhouette of the scene acts as a banner or flag that gives hope to the warriors below. In the end, through the righteousness of the people who are fighting and through the intercession of those on the hilltop, God's blessings are with the people of Israel, and they win the battle.

Moses builds an altar in thanksgiving and calls the place *Adonai-nissi,* which can be translated as "the Lord is my banner" or "the Lord is my miracle." By building this altar and naming the place, Moses not only records this event in the memory of the Israelites but also proclaims to all nations that God is the Lord and that the Israelites are God's people.

The battle with the Amalekites is also fought on the personal level. It indicates a new determination to continue the journey and to do battle with any enemy that tries to obstruct the way. The attitude is no longer one of indifference toward sin but rather of determination to fight against the demons that lurk alongside, or even inside, one's self. Even failure and sin do not discourage the person as they formerly did.

At this stage of the journey, a certain promptness in picking oneself up from sin is possible. A proper speed for repentance is described in Ezek. 1:14: ". . . The living creatures darted to and fro, like a flash of lightning." If one falls into sin, repentance follows immediately, as a "flash of lightning." In this manner, discouragement is combated, and the enemy weakened.

Reflection and Journal-writing Exercises

Poor Moses! The people of Israel give him no peace. Like the father with his demanding little boy on his shoulders, Moses must feel that the people are never satisfied.

1. Relax. Open your mind and heart. When have you felt like Moses—felt that despite your best efforts, people have not been satisfied? Let these recollections come back to you with all the feelings that are part of them.
- Who was there?
- What happened?
- Why were your efforts rebuffed?
- How did you react?
- Did you call on God or try to fix things on your own?
- If you did not call on God, why not?
- If you did call on God, what help did you receive?

2. In your journal, name some of the Amalekites in yourself. Some possibilities are impatience, fretfulness, pride, frivolity, laziness, impetuosity, fear of the future, self-doubt, and self-hate.

Who is Amalek, their leader? *Amalek* is another name for your root sin. Your root sin is the one that is most abiding and, when in control, prompts an attack by the other demons that may be lurking. Discover and name your Amalek. To recognize your root sin is to strike a mortal blow to all the enemies that live along the way of your journey. Do not hesitate to ask a spiritual director or friend to help you identify it.

3. Name the faithful ones in yourself. They represent those parts of yourself that rise up to do battle with the enemies that would keep you from your journey. Who is the Moses, or the leader, among them?

4. In your journal, write a letter from your Moses to your Amalek. State the intention to do battle. Describe your strategies.

5. Moses, even following God's commands, needs help from Aaron and Hur, who hold up his arms. Friends and mentors support us in times of battle. We need them.
• Who are the two most important people in your life journey—the two people who hold up your arms in battle until victory? Who salves your wounds and assists your healing?
• Call these two people to mind—your Aaron and your Hur.
• Recall the battles during which they supported you.
• Thank God for them in a prayer.

Memory Verse

Take this verse with you in your heart and on your lips:

Thou art my hiding place and my shield;
I hope in thy word.

(Ps. 119:114)

PE: *The letter* pe *means "mouth." Pe has two forms, one that curls in on itself, alluding to a closed mouth and silent contemplation, and one that is open and long, symbolizing an open mouth proclaiming the wonders of God.*

Recounting the Deeds of God

Chapter 18 of Exodus describes a beautiful reunion between Moses and his father-in-law, Jethro. Their conversation is about all the marvels the Lord has done for Moses and the people. Sharing the memory of all that has happened charges the atmosphere with God's presence. Jethro exclaims, "'Now I know that the LORD is greater than all gods. . . .'" He offers a burnt offering and sacrifices to God; a banquet is held, and Moses receives counsel.

This meditation focuses on the importance of spiritual conversations. Doing God's will is important, but shared reflection and meditation on God's marvels are equally important. Note that during the conversation, Moses and Jethro take turns being spiritual guides for each other.

Exodus 18:1–24

Jethro, the priest of Midian, Moses' father-in-law, heard of all that God had done for Moses and for Israel [the] people, how the LORD had brought Israel out of Egypt. . . . Moses went out to meet his father-in-law, and did obeisance and kissed him; and they asked each other of their welfare, and went into the tent. Then Moses told his father-in-law all that the LORD had done to Pharaoh and to the Egyptians for Israel's sake, all the hardship that had come upon them in the way, and how the LORD had delivered them. And Jethro rejoiced for all the good which the LORD had done to Israel, in that he had delivered them out of the hand of the Egyptians.

And Jethro said, "Blessed be the LORD, who has delivered you out of the hands of the Egyptians and out of the hand of Pharaoh. Now I know that the LORD is greater than all gods, because [God] delivered the people from under the hand of the Egyptians, when they dealt arrogantly with them." And Jethro, Moses' father-in-law, offered a burnt offering and sacrifices to God; and Aaron came with all the elders of Israel to eat bread with Moses' father-in-law before God.

On the morrow Moses sat to judge the people, and the people stood about Moses from morning till evening. When Moses' father-in-law saw all that he was doing for the people, he said, "What is this that you are doing for the people? Why do you sit alone, and all the people stand about you from morning till evening? . . . What you are doing is not good. You and the people with you will wear yourselves out, for the thing is too heavy for you; you are not able to perform it alone. Listen now to my voice; I will give you counsel, and God be with you! . . . If you do this, and God so commands you, then you will be able to endure, and all this people also will go to their place in peace."

So Moses gave heed to the voice of his father-in-law and did all that he had said.

Commentary

We meet Jethro several times in the Exodus story with several different names: *Reuel, Jether, Jethro,* and *Hobab.* He is a committed religious person possessing the virtues of wisdom and hospitality. He provides Moses with shelter in his escape from Egypt;

he gives Moses his daughter, Zipporah, in marriage; and he looks after Zipporah and the two sons when Moses stays in Egypt to bargain with Pharaoh over the release of the captive Israelites.

Jethro appears in this chapter of Exodus as a man attuned to the works of God and acquainted with all that God has done for Moses and Israel. When he hears that Moses is approaching, he goes to meet Moses where he is encamped near the mountain of God. Jethro takes with him Moses' wife and the two sons. The second son, whom we meet for the first and only time in the biblical narrative, is named Eliezer, meaning "My God is help."

When Moses hears that his father-in-law is coming, Moses goes forward to greet him. The joyful welcome occurs at the mountain of God. This is the same mountain where Moses met God in the burning bush and where he was commissioned to return to Israel to deliver the people. He is now returning with his mission accomplished. After the two men embrace and kiss each other, they enter the tent and Moses tells Jethro all that the Lord has done, including the hardships that came along the way and how the Lord delivered them. To all of this, Jethro exclaims, "'Now I know that the LORD is greater than all gods.'" He then offers a burnt offering and sacrifices to God and sets out a banquet for Moses, Aaron, and the elders of the people.

We learn from this encounter between Moses and Jethro that sharing stories of God's gracious deeds is important. In the telling and retelling, memories are kept alive, an identity as a people is maintained, and hope for the future is built. Without storytelling, the wonders of God's gracious deeds would be forgotten; people would lose their identity. With no memory of God's mercy and justice, they would have no hope for the future.

We are again reminded of how important it is to reinforce the memory with rituals of blessing and thanksgiving. Jewish custom perpetuates the importance of prayers of blessing and thanksgiving in daily life. Blessings have been instituted for every occasion. The blessing always begins, "Blessed are you, LORD our God, Ruler of the Universe, for [here one mentions the specific gift for which thanks is offered]."

Special gifts include everything that exists and happens: fruit growing on trees, fruit growing on the ground, wine, bread, a new house, new clothes, meeting a sage, and so on. God is blessed not only for the good but for bad happenings as well: "Blessed are You, LORD our God, Ruler of the Universe, for [earthquakes, thunder, storms, lightning, and so on]."

Blessing and thanking God are also crucial to Christian prayer, which has its roots in Jewish prayer. The prayers of blessing over the bread and wine at the Christian Eucharist were originally Jewish blessings over bread and wine. The Our Father (more appropriately called the Disciple's Prayer) is similar to the *Amidah,* a daily prayer of the synagogue consisting of a series of eighteen short petitions, each petition a blessing in itself.

The day after their meeting, Jethro watches Moses as he sits and judges the people. When he sees all that Moses is doing for the people, he is astounded. He knows that it is not right, that it is not God's will for one person to work so hard. Moved by the Spirit of God, he counsels Moses. Moses, the man of God, listens to Jethro. He knows that he has no monopoly on God's word. His soul has been attuned to listening for God's voice in all places and events, in the good and in the bad, from his own people and from the people of other nations.

The means by which God speaks to us are not limited. At any moment someone may bring us a message from God. We must be alert for the messenger and try to discern God's voice in the message. This does not necessarily mean, of course, that everyone claiming to have a message from God for us does have one. After listening and trying to discern carefully, we need to decide if the message is from God or not.

Jethro's admonition is also one that all leaders, especially religious leaders, need to hear. Religious leaders often act like Moses does in this scene. In their zeal, they overwork, either because they do not trust in the abilities of others or because they have an exaggerated opinion of their own importance. When this tendency creeps into our life, God sends a prophet to warn us of the danger. The prophet may be a spiritual guide, a friend, a child, or even someone we dislike.

Reflection and Journal-writing Exercises

The Scriptures (Deut. 6:7) alert us to the times and places in which we should speak of God and God's words: ". . . Talk of them when you sit in your house, and when you walk by the way, and when you lie down, and when you rise"—in other words, at all times.

1. Recall a time when you talked about God with another person.
- Who did you talk to?
- What prompted the conversation?
- What was the setting in which the conversation took place?
- Why did you seek this person out?
- How did you feel during and after the talk?
- Do you regularly talk with a Jethro, a spiritual guide? If not, converse with God about your need for a Jethro.
- If you decide that you need a Jethro, talk to God about those areas of your life about which you should seek counsel from your Jethro.

2. Read the following sentence several times: You will wear yourself out, for the thing is too heavy for you; you are not able to do it alone.
- Name one or two areas of your life where you may need someone's—maybe God's—help because going it alone is too heavy a burden.
- Recall in detail one of these burdens.
- Why have you not asked for help from a Jethro or from God? Why do you feel that you must carry the burden alone?
- Reflect on someone who might be your Jethro.
- Imagine going to this person for counsel. Converse with your Jethro about your burden.
- Resolve on some course of counsel so that you do not have to carry your burden alone. Remember that allowing someone to help you is giving them the gift of your confidence and trust.

3. In your journal, write a letter to a Jethro friend.
- Tell this person all that God has done for you.
- Describe the hardships that have come upon you and how God delivered you.
- Close your letter with a prayer that follows the format of a blessing prayer: begin with a blessing, follow with a petition, and close with thanksgiving.

Memory Verse

Take this verse with you in your heart and on your lips:

> With open mouth I pant,
> because I long for thy commandments.
>
> (Ps. 119:131)

KOF: *The letter* kof *stands for* Qadhosh, *or "Holy, Holy, Holy." God is the All-holy One before whom we bow down with the angels and saints chanting "Holy, Holy, Holy, Lord. Heaven and earth are full of your glory." In the curve of* kof *you can see God bending tenderly toward you, and in the vertical bar, your own self reaching upward to God.*

Unto the Mountain of God

The Israelites draw near to the mountain to which they have been called. Their long journey has changed them. They have been purified, their vision is clearer, and their will is stronger. They have come to know God in all God's mighty works on their behalf. Now, standing before the holy mountain, they undergo further purification in preparation for receiving the intensity of divine illumination and the promise of a deeper intimacy with God.

Meditation 16 focuses on the elements of purgation contained in several key phrases: *Israel encamped, you have seen, if you will obey my voice,* and *take heed.*

In meditation 17, illumination is seen as a brilliant light streaming from the mountaintop—an infused wisdom that translates into laws for holy living. God gives the great commandment: "I am the Lord your God, who brought you out of the land of bondage."

In meditation 18, the Israelites move from illumination toward union with God. The people's unconditional surrender to God is ritualized in the betrothal and the nuptial ceremonies. The continuing sign of the betrothal is the Sabbath, and the terms of the covenant are the commandments of love.

On a personal level, a union with God turns all burdens, all spiritual obligations, and all dos and musts into acts of love. The commandments are no longer obligations imposed from without but rather expressions of a loving commitment to the All-holy One. People in union with God seek ways to be holy like God—honest, true, righteous, merciful, compassionate. Prayer is not a duty but a need; without it they cannot live. They seek purity of life, hunger to know God's will, and thirst for union with God.

As you meditate on the following passages from the Scriptures, you will realize that the moments of greatest union with God are also the moments of greatest love of neighbor and of self and that they include a call to serve in building a world of justice and love.

KAPH: Kaph *symbolizes the palm of a hand and a cup (kos). A hand that blesses is like a cup filled to overflowing.*

Purgation

The Israelites have finally arrived at the mountain of God, the mountain where Moses first encountered God at the burning bush. Even though the people have been purified by their long trek through the desert, they are not yet pure enough to meet God face to face. They need further purification at the foot of the mountain. In this meditation, you will seek the purgation experienced by the Israelites and pray with the psalmist,

> Purge me with hyssop, and I shall be clean;
> wash me, and I shall be whiter than snow.
>
> (Ps. 51:7)

Exodus 19:1–15

On the third new moon after the people of Israel had gone forth out of the land of Egypt, on that day they came into the wilderness of Sinai. And when they set out from Rephidim and came into the wilderness of Sinai, they en-camped in the wilderness; and there Israel encamped before the mountain. And Moses went up to God, and the LORD called to him out of the mountain, saying, "Thus you shall say to the house of Jacob, and tell the people of Israel: You have seen what I did to the Egyptians, and how I bore you on eagles' wings and brought you to myself. Now therefore, if you will obey my voice and keep my covenant, you shall be my own possession among all peoples; for all the earth is mine, and you shall be to me a kingdom of priests and a holy nation. These are the words which you shall speak to the children of Israel."

So Moses came and called the elders of the people, and set before them all these words which the LORD had commanded him. And all the people answered together and said, "All that the LORD has spoken we will do." And Moses reported the words of the people to the LORD. And the LORD said to Moses, "Lo, I am coming to you in a thick cloud, that the people may hear when I speak with you, and may also believe you for ever."

Then Moses told the words of the people to the LORD. And the LORD said to Moses, "Go to the people and consecrate them today and tomorrow, and let them wash their garments, and be ready by the third day; for on the third day the LORD will come down upon Mount Sinai in the sight of all the people. And you shall set bounds for the people round about, saying, 'Take heed that you do not go up into the mountain or touch the border of it; whoever touches the mountain shall be put to death; no hand shall touch [that person], but [such a one] shall be stoned or shot; whether beast or [human], [they] shall not live.' When the trumpet sounds a long blast, they shall come up to the mountain." So Moses went down from the mountain to the people, and consecrated the people; and they washed their garments. And he said to the people, "Be ready by the third day. . . ."

Commentary

When Moses first encountered God in the burning bush at Sinai, the Lord cautioned, "'Do not come near; put off your shoes from your feet, for the place on which you are standing is holy ground.'" Now on his return to the mountain, purified and strong, Moses goes up the mountain and talks to God: "And Moses went up to God." The people, however, are not allowed, nor able, to go up the mountain. They will hear God

speak, but they must be purified even more "'and be ready by
the third day; for on the third day the LORD will come down
upon Mount Sinai in the sight of all the people.'"

The ways of purgation, which have taken place and will
continue to take place in the lives of the people, are indicated
in several key phrases in the passage from the Scriptures: *Israel
encamped, you have seen, if you will obey my voice,* and *take heed.*

The word *encamped* points to the purifying process of waiting for God and intuiting God's presence. Revelation, whether
divine or human, is always a gift and never can be presumed or
demanded; so the people pitch their tents to wait for God and
concentrate on hearing God's voice.

How did the Israelites know where and when to attend to
God? How did they recognize their holy meeting place? The
stories of Abraham and Samuel give us the clues.

In both cases—Abraham's recognition of the mountain to
which he is to take his son, Isaac, and Samuel's recognition of
God's call—recognition is preceded by obedience, an obedience
that is marked by a responsive trust and openness. It sharpens
inner alertness to the unseen and allows an inner knowing that
those without trust and openness are incapable of having. This
obedience is gained through the purifying power of God at
work in the human journey.

Like Abraham and Samuel, the Israelites went through such
a purifying, growing process. While they were enslaved in
Egypt, their capacity to hear or see the Divine was dulled. While
held in bondage, an impenetrable barrier between them and
their God existed. But having been delivered and purified and
cleansed, they are awakened to the signs of transcendence
around and within themselves.

So when God says to the people, "'You have seen what I did
. . . and how I bore you on eagles' wings and brought you to
myself,'" we know that the people have undergone a purifying
and sensitizing process. God has been like a mother eagle training her eaglets to fly. Like a mother eagle who pushes each eaglet onto her outstretched wings, hurls it into the sky, catches

it, and repeats the performance until the eaglet knows how to fly, so has God carried and trained the people. The lessons have been hard, but because of these painful lessons in flying freely, the people have arrived at the foot of the mountain.

The importance of obedience in the purifying process is evident: "If you obey you shall always be my special possession. You shall be to me a kingdom of priests and a holy nation."

The closer the people are to God, the more crucial their obedience becomes. They are told not to go onto the mountain before they are readied. The Divine Presence is so intense there that it is a refining fire burning out every impurity and burning up those to whom impurities are still attached.

One final cleansing must be undertaken—a cleansing that will enable a total and complete turning to God. The people must wash their clothes as a sign of their willingness to undergo this cleansing—as a sign of their total obedience to God.

All of these stages of purgation are part of the preparation for witnessing the descent of God upon the mountain on the third day. First, they encamp and wait for God. Second, they are further sensitized to the signs of transcendence. Third, they are reminded of the importance of obedience. Finally, they must refrain from anything that might distract their total attention to God and must undergo a final purification.

Anyone who arrives at the foot of the mountain and is encamped there has been on a long journey, a journey from the self enslaved and bound in its own selfishness to the self that through God's grace has taken hold of its own life and reached a place that borders on divine ground. Figuratively, immense distances have been traveled; even chronologically, the journey might have taken a long time. Tremendous growth and spiritual maturation, far outstripping any natural maturation, has taken place. Even so, arrival at the foot of the mountain can still be a time of immense pain because of the remaining, deeply rooted impurities that can barely stand the intense heat and light of the divine radiance. It will take all of the built-up trust in God's eaglelike care to endure the purification that still must take place.

Reflection and Journal-writing Exercises

1. Before praying or continuing this meditation, wash your face and hands slowly and carefully to ritually remind yourself of approaching God in purity of heart and openness. As you do so, repeat these words: Wash me, O God, and I shall be whiter than snow.

2. Now, sit quietly. Relax. Repeat over and over the beautiful, reassuring words of Yahweh: "'I bore you on eagle's wings and brought you to myself.'" Imagine being borne on God's back:
- What do you see?
- Where are you going?
- What do you feel?
- What do you say to God?

3. Recall times when you experienced the four stages of purification:
- a time of encampment, when you waited for God's presence and voice
- a time when you sensed God's presence and knew you were near holy ground
- a time when you were ready to obey whatever God might ask
- a time when you were ready to step onto holy ground but knew that final purification was still necessary

4. Imagine yourself at the foot of the holy mountain anticipating God's descent to you:
- What purifications have taken place that make you ready to meet God face to face?
- What final purification is still needed?

5. In your journal, write a greeting prayer that you would use when meeting God face to face at this moment in your life journey.

Memory Verse

Take this verse with you in your heart and on your lips:

> For I have become like a wineskin in the smoke,
>   yet I have not forgotten thy statutes.
>
> (Ps. 119:83)

ALEPH: Aleph *is the first letter of the word* anokhi, *"I." "'I am the* LORD *your God.'"* Aleph *has an arm pointing upward and a leg pointing downward. God, who transcends the earth, is also present to it.*

Illumination

God descends upon Mount Sinai, like a teacher to a classroom, to instruct the Israelites on the terms of the covenant that is to bind them with God forever. Like students before their teacher, the people are encamped at the foot of the mountain. The opening of class is dramatic: thunder and lightning, fire and smoke, a thick cloud, and a loud and long trumpet blast. The teachings given by God to the Israelites are the most important teachings humankind has ever received.

The light emanating from them continues to illuminate the minds of millions of people in our time. Because these teachings have been heard so many times, there is real danger of taking them for granted or of looking elsewhere for illumination. Ask God to give you a fresh mind and a new heart with which to approach the instructions of God:

> Open my eyes, that I may behold
> wondrous things out of thy law.

> (Ps. 119:18)

Exodus 19:16—20:7

On the morning of the third day there were thunders and lightnings, and a thick cloud upon the mountain, and a very loud trumpet blast, so that all the people who were in the camp trembled. Then Moses brought the people out of the camp to meet God; and they took their stand at the foot of the mountain. And Mount Sinai was wrapped in smoke, because the LORD descended upon it in fire; and the smoke of it went up like the smoke of a kiln, and the whole mountain quaked greatly. And as the sound of the trumpet grew louder and louder, Moses spoke, and God answered him in thunder. And the LORD came down upon Mount Sinai, to the top of the mountain. . . .

And God spoke all these words, saying,

"I am the LORD your God, who brought you out of the land of Egypt, out of the house of bondage.

"You shall have no other gods before me.

"You shall not make for yourself a graven image, or any likeness of anything that is in heaven above, or that is in the earth beneath, or that is in the water under the earth; you shall not bow down to them or serve them; for I the LORD your God am a jealous God, visiting the iniquity of the [ancestors] upon the children to the third and the fourth generation of those who hate me, but showing steadfast love to thousands of those who love me and keep my commandments.

"You shall not take the name of the LORD your God in vain; for the LORD will not hold [you] guiltless [if you take God's] name in vain.

Commentary

Familiarity with these scriptural verses often prevents us from probing deeper into their mystery. The following three questions might provoke you to see new things in the text:

1. Doesn't it seem odd for the Scriptures to state, "Then Moses brought the people out of the camp to meet God; and they took their stand at the foot of the mountain," when God has been with them during their entire journey?

2. Why would the Scriptures tell us that "the sound of the trumpet blast grew louder and louder"? Normally, the longer a person blows a horn, the weaker and fainter the sound becomes. But here it grows increasingly stronger.
3. The people's response to God's word is, "All that the Lord has spoken we will do and we will obey." Why might the phrase *we will do* be placed before *we will obey?*

First, what is striking about the scriptural statement in number 1 is that God is already at the mountain when the people arrive even though God accompanied them on their journey from Egypt. God is present when Israel leaves Egypt and present when Israel arrives at Mount Sinai. In the words of the psalmist,

> The LORD will keep
> > your *going out* and your *coming in*
> > from this time forth and for evermore.
> > > (Ps. 121:8 [Emphasis added.])

The prophet Ezekiel has a similar experience:

> And the *hand of the LORD* was *there upon me;* and [God] said to me, "Arise, go forth into the plain, and there I will speak with you." So I arose and went forth into the plain; and, lo, *the glory of the LORD stood there.* . . . (Ezek. 3:22–23 [Emphasis added.])

From the simple phrase "Moses brought the people out of the camp to meet God," we are reminded again that the God who commands us to go forward and accompanies us is also there to meet us in an even more intimate way when we arrive at our destination.

The second half of the sentence, "and they took their stand at the foot of the mountain," has been the subject of many different interpretations. In one of these interpretations, God uproots the mountain from its place in the earth and arches it over the people like a cask, saying, "If you accept my Torah, well and good, but if not, there your grave will be." The frightened people cry out, "Yes, yes. All that the Lord has spoken we will do." Such a story points to the level of intimacy between the people and God. A people that have come to know God's love and their own weaknesses trust that God will see to it that they carry out the divine will. The commandments are seen as God obliging Israel's most noble instincts by reinforcing its desire with compulsion.

Second, the notion of the horn growing louder rather than weaker indicates that the Israelites are getting more attuned to God's voice. At first God is heard speaking softly. As the people's ability and perception increase, so does the sound and volume of God's voice. Such a phenomenon is contained in two lines of poetry written by e. e. cummings:

(now the ears of my ears awake and
now the eyes of my eyes are opened)

(*100 Selected Poems*, p. 114)

Third, the people respond to all of God's words by replying, "Whatever the Lord speaks we will do and we will obey." Some understanding of Hebrew opens a new door into the meaning of this phrase. The Hebrew word for *obey* comes from the root word for *listen*, so the sentence is also translated as "Whatever the Lord speaks we will do and we will listen." First do and then listen. Would it not be more logical for these human beings with free will to listen first and then judge whether to carry out the commands? Such an answer would make the people's response conditional. The reverse order, which gives priority to doing over listening, means that the Israelites pledge their absolute, unconditional commitment to God even before they know what the commandments and their implications will be.

The first commandment sounds more like a declaration than a commandment: "'I am the Lord your God, who brought you out of the land of Egypt, out of the house of bondage. You shall have no other gods before me.'" The first part of this declaration can be translated in either of two ways:

• I the Lord . . . am your God, who brought you out of the land of Egypt.
• I . . . am the Lord your God, who brought you out of the land of Egypt.

Try repeating these sentences to yourself several times according to the breaks indicated by the ellipses. Do you notice the shift in meaning when you change the way you read the sentence?

In the first instance, God says, "I who am called 'the Lord' am alone your God, who watches over you by a special providence, who already brought you out of Egypt." This is a statement about God. In the second instance, God is God because of what God did for the people. Although God was God before, now the people know from their own experience of being brought out of Egypt that God is God. We too, perhaps, know God best by experiencing God in the events of our life rather than by simply hearing declarations about God. Both interpretations are possible, and each complements the other.

The words of the declaration read, "I am the Lord your God, who brought you out of Egypt," not "I am the Lord your God, who created you, who made heaven and earth." The emphasis in Exodus is on experience of God versus hearing the story of Creation.

The second part of the declaration is the command "'You shall have no other gods before me.'" This part of the declaration guarantees the truth of the opening. To have any other gods but God is slavery. Obeying this command exchanges the fears and anxieties that torment those subject to finite gods for the fear of God, who removes all other fears.

Despite the command, the temptation to worship other gods remains. Idolatry includes not only the devoting of all energies and thoughts to the accumulation of wealth and achievement but also the objects of religion that replace God. The holiest of words or acts can be false images of God if they are used to control and oppress people.

The commandments are expressions of infused wisdom and are a norm by which to judge faithfulness to the covenant with God. They are received as a communication of light, an inner knowing—not necessarily intellectual, theoretical knowledge but living knowledge, a wisdom that translates into holy living. What is received would be expressed in phrases like "Great things were shown to me," "I learned so many things in an instant," and "Now I see."

Reflection and Journal-writing Exercises

1. Imagine yourself with the people at Mount Sinai as you reread the biblical text. Certain passages or words will light up. Whenever a word or phrase lights up, even slightly, stay with it, repeating it over and over. Keep repeating that word or phrase until its light shines into your mind or heart. You will know when this happens, for either your heart will be warmed or your mind enlightened.

2. Record in your journal the words and phrases that attracted you. If possible, write out any personal commandments that they suggest to you.

3. Close your meditation by writing a prayer, blessing God for having infused you with divine light and wisdom.

Memory Verse

Take this verse with you in your heart and on your lips:

Blessed are those . . .
    who walk in the law of the LORD!

(Ps. 119:1)

MEDITATION 18

ZAYIN: *Zayin, the seventh letter of the Hebrew alphabet with a numerical value of seven, stands for* Sabbath, *the seventh day; for* zakar, *meaning "remember"; and for* tsachor, *meaning "light."*

Covenant and Union

In this meditation, you will reflect on the Sabbath, which is a gift of time, and on the terms of the covenant, which have more to do with deeds than with words. Because the covenant is a covenant of love between God and the people, all the deeds of the agreement are related to love and justice.

If you read all the laws of the covenant, as Moses read them all to the people, you will see that they are based on strict justice. The covenant norm of an eye for an eye, a tooth for a tooth, and a hand for a hand might seem harsh, but it represents a great advance in human relations from the time when revenge was the norm.

Exodus 20:8—24:8

"Remember the sabbath day, to keep it holy. Six days you shall labor, and do all your work; but the seventh day is a sabbath to the LORD your God; in it you shall not do any work, you, or your son, or your daughter, your manservant, or your maidservant, or your cattle, or the sojourner who is within your gates; for in six days the LORD made heaven and earth, the sea, and all that is in them, and rested the seventh day; therefore the LORD blessed the sabbath day and hallowed it.

"Honor your father and your mother, that your days may be long in the land which the LORD your God gives you.

"You shall not kill.

"You shall not commit adultery.

"You shall not steal.

"You shall not bear false witness against your neighbor.

"You shall not covet your neighbor's house.". . .

. . . And Moses wrote all the words of the LORD. And he rose early in the morning, and built an altar at the foot of the mountain. . . . Then he took the book of the covenant, and read it in the hearing of the people; and they said, "All that the LORD has spoken we will do, and we will be obedient." And Moses took the blood and threw it upon the people, and said, "Behold the blood of the covenant which the LORD has made with you in accordance with all these words."

Commentary

The sabbath commandment is the only one in the decalogue that addresses ritual worship of God; all the other commandments refer to relationships between human persons. The purpose of the Sabbath is stated clearly in Exod. 31:16–17: "'Therefore the people of Israel shall keep the sabbath . . . as a perpetual covenant. It is a sign for ever between me and the people of Israel. . . .'"

To keep the Sabbath is to imitate God. In the creation of the world, God worked for six days and rested on the seventh. Our mode of operation is to be the same, six days of work and one day of rest. By imitating God in living the rhythm and alternation of six days of work and one day of rest, we become co-creators with God, keeping our world alive like the rhythmic pulsing of the heart does the human body. The seven-day week with its six-to-one cadence of work and rest is a creative, energizing unit of time.

The remaining six of the Ten Commandments, beginning with "'Honor your father and your mother,'" show us how to love our neighbor. Love of God and love of neighbor are interwoven. We cannot love God without loving God's Creation. A gauge with which to measure our love of God is our love of neighbor.

Love of neighbor begins close to home—with love of our parents. This is the only commandment that has a blessing attached to it: "'that your days may be long.'" A long life does not necessarily mean life lived chronologically. It means quality time, a life that is rich and full.

The positive command to honor our parents is followed by a negative command, not to murder or kill. The Hebrew word for *murder* is *retsach,* meaning "to kill with evil intent." Included in the prohibition is the command not to destroy either one's own or another person's self, that is, another person's self-image, good name, honor, or dignity.

The commandments concerned with adultery and stealing refer not only to sexual irresponsibility and the stealing of physical goods but to forms of inner activity as well; ideas, emotions, loyalties, and commitments can also be prostituted or stolen.

Contained in the commandment to refrain from bearing false witness is the command to shun all forms of lying, not only to and about one's neighbor but also to and about oneself.

The tenth commandment, concerning coveting, applies not only to another's property but to the whole of Creation. The world and all that is in it belongs to God. The proper attitude toward the world and the goods of the world should be one of gratitude for gifts received from a bountiful and caring God rather than one of greed and covetousness.

All of the commandments can be summarized in the one word *love,* love of God and love of neighbor (Deut. 6:4–9; Lev. 19:17–18; Mark 12:29–31). When the Israelites left Egypt, they could not have heard these commandments. They were so full of the bitterness and oppression of slavery that the promptings of their inner spirit were choked and blocked. The life they lived in the desert had a purifying effect. They began to breathe clean air and to know the existence of other and better worlds. Meeting God at the foot of the mountain was a final cleansing that opened them to deep feelings of healing and compassion, of love and forgiveness. Their inner spirit was formerly the home of a thousand fears and doubts. Now their spirit is as clean and empty as the vast desert they have traversed. They are open to God and God's word.

The final uniting of the people is accomplished. They have become a people with unique obligations to God and to one another. The creation of a people out of a group of individual slaves who were alienated from one another and the bonding of this people to God are now facts. Their reality is sealed in blood. Moses takes the blood of the sacrificial offerings and dashes half of it against the altar, symbolically committing God to the covenant, and then he throws the other half on the people, saying, "'Behold the blood of the covenant which the LORD has made with you in accordance with all these words.'"

Even when we are secure in the knowledge that God has chosen us, loves us, life does not suddenly become perfect. Sin and evil continue to exist, but our attitude toward the world is different. If our desires are centered on God, we can perceive the world without wanting to possess it. Because we can let go, we are free. When we willingly step into the transforming flame of God's presence, we take on a new mode of being in which human dichotomies (life and death, good and evil) become paradoxes that are reconciled in an infinite wholeness.

Reflection and Journal-writing Exercises

1. Compose in your journal a personal covenant with God.
- What are the terms?
- What does God promise you?

- What do you promise God?
- What role does the Sabbath have in your covenant with God?

2. Examine the level of your intimacy with God by applying the gauge of the commandments:
- Is God the Lord your God?
- Is your will in harmony with God's will?
- Do you wish always and everywhere to do and listen to God's commands?
- Are there strange gods in your life? If so, list all of them and try to describe how and why you worship them.
- Do you keep the Sabbath? Do you look forward to the Sabbath as a day for the Lord and for rest?
- Are you faithful to prayer every day?
- What is your relationship with other people? Do you hold resentment against anyone? Does any bitterness or envy reside in your heart? Do you find yourself blessing and thanking God and others for their goodness? Do you protect the names of those who are maligned? Are you honest and truthful?
- Finally, does this list sound burdensome? Does it contain ways of behavior you have embraced?

3. To experience union with God is to desire union with others, the self, and the whole universe. Terms like *them-us, superior-inferior,* and *win-lose* are replaced by phrases like *we, together-with,* and *win-win.*
- Recall times when you talked and acted in terms of them-us, superior-inferior, and win-lose. What kind of events were they? Who were the people involved? To what extent was God present during these times?
- Recall times when you talked and acted in terms of we, together-with, and win-win. What kind of events were they? Who were the people involved? To what extent was God present during these times?

4. In your journal, record those times when closeness to God prompted you to have new regard for and closeness to a human person. Write a prayer of thanksgiving for the gift of these times.

Memory Verse

Take this verse with you in your heart and on your lips:

> Remember thy word to thy servant,
>   in which thou hast made me hope.
>
> (Ps. 119:49)

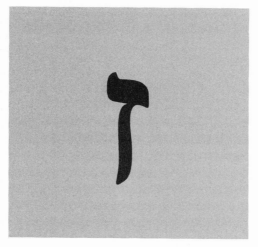

ZAYIN: *The letter* zayin *stands for* tsachor, *or "light." God is the Light of the world. When we obey God and walk according to God's commandments, we walk in the light. If you look closely at this letter, you can see light streaming toward earth from the throne of God.*

Ascending the Mountain

Clouds of light swirl about the mountain of God. At times the bright light pierces through the darkness; at other times, the darkness overwhelms the light.

The people, having received the terms of the covenant and having promised undying fidelity, are invited to ascend the mountain. "Come up to me," God invites. The ascent unto God is met by a descent of God. The meeting creates an indwelling of the person in God and of God in the person, during which the instruction "Build me a sanctuary that I may dwell among you" is given (meditation 19).

The brightness of God's radiance is obscured by the clouds of human darkness. Stumbling and losing their way, the people fall into idolatry. But again they are rescued by a new revelation of God's mercy and a renewal of the covenant (meditation 20). What could have ended in tragedy ends in triumph. A chastened understanding of what it means to be human is realized: to be human is to be a traveler journeying both in God's light from the mountaintops and in the valleys of human shadows. The human shadows persist, but the light of God continues to pierce them (meditation 21).

TETH: Teth, *which has one arm reaching up-ward and the other arm folded inward, represents a person who is ascending closer and closer to God.* Teth *also stands for* tobh, *meaning "good." It is good to be alive and good to give thanks to the Lord.*

Ascent

In the dramatic encounter at Sinai, the terms of the covenant were drawn up and the covenant between God and Israel sealed. As in the marriage covenant, this covenant is meant to be a dynamic relationship that deepens with the living out of the mutual promises that are made.

In the scriptural text for this meditation, the words "Come up to me" are repeated in various ways. Moses and members of the community respond to the invitation, ascending higher and higher into the divine mystery. Moses alone is allowed to ascend into the very presence of God, where he is given further understanding of the terms of the covenant and instructions for the building of the sanctuary. When his time of instruction is over, he will return down the mountain to teach others the ways of God and to give them instructions on how they are to build a sanctuary of God.

Pray for the grace to ascend closer to God and for an understanding of what it means to become a living sanctuary of the most-high God:

> To thee, O Lord, I lift up my soul. Lead me in thy truth and teach me.

Exodus 24:1—25:14

And [God] said to Moses, "Come up to the LORD, you and Aaron, Nadab, and Abihu, and seventy of the elders of Israel, and worship afar off. Moses alone shall come near to the LORD; but the others shall not come near, and the people shall not come up with him.". . .

Then Moses and Aaron, Nadab, and Abihu, and seventy of the elders of Israel went up, and they saw the God of Israel; and there was under [God's] feet as it were a pavement of sapphire stone, like the very heaven for clearness. And [God] did not lay [a] hand on the [elders] of the people of Israel; they beheld God, and ate and drank.

The LORD said to Moses, "Come up to me on the mountain, and wait there; and I will give you the tables of stone, with the law and the commandment, which I have written for their instruction." So Moses rose with his servant Joshua, and Moses went up into the mountain of God. And he said to the elders, "Tarry here for us, until we come to you again; and, behold, Aaron and Hur are with you; whoever has a cause, [they must] go to them."

Then Moses went up on the mountain, and the cloud covered the mountain. The glory of the LORD settled on Mount Sinai, and the cloud covered it six days; and on the seventh day [God] called to Moses out of the midst of the cloud. Now the appearance of the glory of the LORD was like a devouring fire on the top of the mountain in the sight of the people of Israel. And Moses entered the cloud, and went up on the mountain. And Moses was on the mountain forty days and forty nights.

The LORD said to Moses, "Speak to the people of Israel. . . . And let them make me a sanctuary, that I may dwell in their midst. According to all that I show you concerning the pattern of the tabernacle, and of all its furniture, so you shall make it.

"They shall make an ark of acacia wood. . . . You shall make poles of acacia wood, and overlay them with gold. And you shall put the poles into the rings on the sides of the ark, to carry the ark by them.

Commentary

This chapter of Exodus is a story of ascents. A large group begins the ascent of the mountain, but not all of the members ascend to the same height. At one level, the elders are told to wait with Aaron and Hur. At a still higher level, Joshua stops. Moses ascends higher than all of them.

At each level of ascent, special benefits are bestowed. At the first level, Moses, Aaron, Nadab, Abihu, and seventy of the elders see the God of Israel. Whatever vision they have, we can tell that a feast is connected to seeing God: "they beheld God, and ate and drank." We can only surmise what kind of heavenly food they eat, a food that will nourish them long after the experience.

At the next level, Joshua stops. The food he receives is not described. We can suppose that his nourishment enables him to become the future leader of the people of Israel.

Moses ascends higher than all the others. He enters into the Presence, into the glory of the Lord, which is like a "devouring fire." For forty days and forty nights, there is silence—profound, deep, mysterious.

When the meeting between God and Moses is finished, Moses brings all of God's further commandments and instructions back to the people. A few examples can help us appreciate the messages contained in these commandments and instructions. One of the commands is to build a sanctuary: "'And let them make me a sanctuary, that I may dwell in their midst.'" This sentence does not say, "Let them make me a sanctuary, that I may dwell in *it*." The use of *in their midst* instead of *in it* indicates that the sanctuary is to be the hearts of the people, for the people are to constitute the temple of God, both as individuals and as a community.

The instructions for building the ark contain more lessons. The ark is to have poles so that it can be carried. God will not remain at Sinai. God is portable. Wherever the covenanted people go, God will go. If this be exile, God will go into exile. If this be the desert, even for forty more years, God will remain in the desert. The same is true of God's word. Because the Ten Commandments are to be placed in the ark, they too are portable. They are not to be restricted to the place where they have been given or to the people to whom they have been given. They are to be for all peoples and for all times.

The directions for building a "mercy seat" or "seat of God's mercy" on top of the ark tell the people something about the purpose of holy places. "'There I will meet with you, and from above the mercy seat, from between the two cherubim that are upon the ark of the testimony, I will speak with you. . . .'" God fixes the location of the Divine Presence on the ark only for the sake of the people. When God's presence is everywhere like air, no one quite knows in which direction to turn to address the Presence. So God restricts the Divine Self, so to speak, to a clearly defined holy place. However, if the people attempt to restrict God to a time or space or image, they clearly profane God, who is "I AM WHO I AM."

God is the ruler of all things, even us. Indeed, we are temples of God, but true worship of God is grounded in justice and in love of neighbor, not in hoarding God's gifts to us. The temples of God are to be used to honor and serve God. God is present in the seat of mercy; God is present in our mercy toward others.

As you come to the end of this meditation, remind yourself of the loftiness of the destiny of your journey, which is to become a living temple of the most-high God—an ascent that has no human limits.

Meditation and Journal-writing Exercises

1. Draw a mountain. Then draw steps ascending the mountain, steps that mark events in your life and that show your ascent unto God. Some steps might be small, some large. Begin on the first step with your first remembrance of God in your life. Then continue marking the ascending steps with major events in your journey toward God. Label each step and describe the event more fully in your journal.

2. On the same drawing, mark those times when a slip, a fall backward, was also the impetus for further ascent.

3. Meeting God can also be seen as descending to meet God in the depths of the inner self. Draw a spiral seashell to represent a descending path.

- Imagine yourself moving along this path to meet God in the innermost center of the seashell. What dimensions of yourself do you meet along the curves and edges of the path? Which ones encourage you to continue to move toward God? Which ones tempt you to turn back? Do some tell you that you have no farther to go? Would you like to remain at some places along the path?
- Imagine now that you see God at the center of the shell. Talk to this all-merciful God about your hopes and fears, your struggles and desires.

Memory Verse

Take this verse with you in your heart and on your lips:

> Thou art good and doest good;
>   teach me thy statutes.
>
> (Ps. 119:68)

HEH: *Heh is a symbol of God and of the human condition. The open bottom of* heh *symbolizes how easy it is to fall into sin, and the tiny space between the left leg and the roof symbolizes that there is always a way through which the sinner may repent and return to God.*

Mercy

The story of the golden calf is a representative story of sin and rebellion in the face of the many favors received from the hand of God. In this meditation, reflect on the sin of idolatry, on repentance, and on the magnitude of God's forgiveness.

Exodus 32:1—34:7

When the people saw that Moses delayed to come down from the mountain, the people gathered themselves together to Aaron, and said to him, "Up, make us gods, who shall go before us; as for this Moses, the [one] who brought us up out of the land of Egypt, we do not know what has become of him." And Aaron said to them, "Take off the rings of gold which are in the ears of your wives, your sons, and your daughters, and bring them to me." So all the people took off the rings of gold which were in their ears, and brought them to Aaron. And he received the gold at their hand, and fashioned it with a graving tool, and made a molten calf; and they said, "These are your gods, O Israel, who brought you up out of the land of Egypt!" . . .

And the LORD said to Moses, "Go down; for your people, whom you brought up out of the land of Egypt, have corrupted themselves; they have turned aside quickly out of the way which I commanded them. . . .

. . . And as soon as [Moses] came near the camp and saw the calf and the dancing, Moses' anger burned hot, and he threw the tables out of his hands and broke them at the foot of the mountain. And he took the calf which they had made, and burnt it with fire, and ground it to powder, and scattered it upon the water, and made the people of Israel drink it. . . .

On the morrow Moses said to the people, "You have sinned a great sin. And now I will go up to the LORD; perhaps I can make atonement for your sin." So Moses returned to the LORD. . . .

The LORD said to Moses, "Cut two tables of stone like the first; and I will write upon the tables the words that were on the first tables, which you broke. Be ready in the morning, and come up in the morning to Mount Sinai, and present yourself there to me on the top of the mountain. No [one] shall come up with you. . . . So Moses cut two tables of stone like the first; and he rose early in the morning and went up on Mount Sinai, as the LORD had commanded him, and took in his hand two tables of stone. And the LORD descended in the cloud and stood with him there, and proclaimed the name of the LORD. The LORD passed before him, and proclaimed, "The LORD, the LORD, a God merciful and gracious, slow to anger, and abounding in steadfast love and faithfulness, keeping steadfast love for thousands, forgiving iniquity and transgression and sin. . . ."

Commentary

The building and worship of the golden calf is a sin greater than any previous sins of the people. Before, when they sinned, it was often through ignorance of God and God's ways. Now, in their infidelity, they turn away from God with the promises of the covenant still fresh on their lips. What prompts such infidelity?

A mixed multitude of people—not only Israelites—came out of Egypt. A variety of people with a variety of motives left with Moses. The promise of freedom had great appeal, and many Egyptians left their country to escape from the past or to find a new kind of future. Motives were mixed, and there were soft spots in the community's faith and commitment to God. During Moses' absence, the leadership of the people is in the hands of an as yet uninitiated Aaron, and without strong leadership, discontented individuals sow suspicion and doubt among the people. When Moses returns, he sees that the people are out of control (because Aaron has let them get out of control) and that they are a menace to any who might oppose them.

We do not ascend to God without struggle. Each ascent to a higher level includes the danger of slipping and falling. The greater the ascent, the greater the fall might be. Fears, fantasies, wild thoughts, and distractions all form obstacles that face anyone about to climb from one level to the next.

While near the mountain, with God in sight and Moses in the lead, the people are single-minded and their path is clear. But when Moses remains hidden at the mountaintop, the people begin to look away from the mountain, the path becomes obscure, and they become confused. They begin to search for other gods.

The Hebrew word for *calf* points out the direction of their search. The word is *eghel,* "young bull," standing for animal vitality and the lower passions. The result is an orgiastic feast far different from the meals they had been sharing in their journey with God. They are rapidly losing the identity they have gained as a people of the one God, who had freed them and joined with them in a covenanted union.

In turning away from God, the people have broken the covenant. The fragments of the tablets are a dramatic demonstration of this bitter reality. But a vital link with God remains in the trust and commitment of Moses. Moses once again takes steps to win God's forgiveness for the people.

These steps include all the ingredients of true repentance, a "turning around" back to God. The first step is to get rid of the golden calf. Moses burns it with fire, a strong purging element. He then takes the ashes, grinds them into fine powder, strews them upon the water, and makes the Israelites drink the ashes mixed with water. The Israelites digest their sin, admitting it and remembering it for the generations to come.

Then Moses calls out, "Whoever is for the Lord, come here." The people must turn about-face and make a new decisive choice for the Lord. To those who have repented, Moses adds, "You are guilty of a great sin. Yet I will now go up to the Lord; perhaps I may win forgiveness for your sin."

Moses climbs the mountain and again enters into the Divine Presence. With the boldness born of love of God and the people, Moses pleads, "Alas, these people are guilty of a great sin in making for themselves a god of gold. Now, if you will forgive their sin, well and good, but if not, erase me from the record that you have written!"

Here Moses is at his greatest; his concern for the people has given him an unusual courage that enables him to stand before the Lord and make demands on their behalf. He argues with God not to give the enemy a chance to accuse the Divine of bringing the people forth only to destroy them in the end. God too must repent. "Turn from your blazing anger," Moses advises, "and renounce the plan to punish your people. Remember your servants Abraham, Isaac, and Jacob." And the Lord does repent. The punishment that had been planned is renounced.

The Lord proclaims the grace and compassion of the Divine Inner Self:

> The Lord! The Lord!
> A God compassionate and gracious, slow to anger
> abounding in kindness and faithfulness,
> extending kindness to the thousandth generation,
> forgiving iniquity, transgression, and sin;
> yet God does not remit all punishment.

This famous statement, coming as it does after the sin of worshiping the golden calf, contains what has come to be known as the Thirteen Attributes of Divine Mercy. The proclamation begins with a repetition of the holy name of God, *Yahweh,* often written *YHWH.* The use of *H* in *YHWH* denotes the attribute of mercy in God. The first *H* is for before a person sins, and the other *H* is for after a person sins. God is merciful both before and after a person sins.

"Yahweh, Yahweh"—two times the ineffable name is pronounced. The first *Yahweh* refers to the removal of God's presence because of sin, and the second *Yahweh* to the presence of God that remains, urging the sinner to repent. "Return," "Come back to me," God's voice calls from within and from without. The sin itself is made the servant of repentance, for it troubles the inner self and makes life miserable.

God forgives the people completely and in doing so reveals another side of God—God's merciful, compassionate, and gracious side. The covenant is renewed, and the renewal makes the covenant stronger and deeper than before the people sinned: "'Behold, I make a covenant. Before all your people I will do marvels, such as have not been wrought in all the earth or in any nation; and all the people among whom you are shall see the work of the LORD. . . .'"

Reflection and Journal-writing Exercises

1. Recall a time when you turned away from God to idols.
- What were the circumstances?
- Who or what was your golden calf?
- Who was involved?
- Was it at a time when you were making great progress in your ascent to God?
- What caused your fidelity to give away?
- Was your inner Moses absent at the time? If so, why?
- In what way did you hear God's voice calling you to return? Was it an inner voice? Another person? An event?

2. Recall a time when another person was a Moses in your repentance and reconciliation.
• What was the sin?
• Who was your Moses?
• What did your Moses do?

3. Reflect on the thirteen attributes of God's mercy: (1) Lord, (2) Lord, (3) a God (4) merciful (5) and gracious, (6) slow to anger, (7) and abounding in steadfast love (8) and faithfulness, (9) keeping steadfast love for thousands, (10) forgiving iniquity (11) and transgression (12) and sin (13) but who will by no means clear the guilty, visiting the iniquity of the ancestors upon the children and the children's children to the third and the fourth generation. (*Note:* This last attribute need not be interpreted as God punishing succeeding generations for the sins of a previous one but rather as the effects of sin lasting for a long time.)
• Pick the attributes in which you have most strongly experienced God's forgiveness.
• In your journal, describe the events and the manner in which God's forgiveness was experienced in those attributes.

Memory Verse

Take this verse with you in your heart and on your lips:

> Incline my heart to thy testimonies,
> and not to gain!

(Ps. 119:36)

NUN: Nun *is for* nephesh, *meaning "soul"; for* niggun, *"melody"; and* ner tamid, *"the sanctuary lamp." The melody of the soul is like a lamp before the Lord.*

Radiance

For another forty days, Moses is hidden away with God on the mountaintop, where he speaks with God as friend to friend. Nearness to God and the touch of God's hand make him as radiant as a hot coal glowing in the midst of a fire. His face glows with light so intense that ordinary people cannot look directly at him.

From a simple shepherd who first met God at the burning bush, Moses has grown into the man of God, filled with divine radiance. Now as never before he is equipped to lead, teach, and show his people God's ways.

This man, Moses, is a reflection of the "I" of our self. Having met God, the "I" of our self can throw light on all the other facets of our personality, even our shadowy sides.

Pray that you will meet God in your inner self so that you may be enlightened, see, and become whole.

Exodus 34:29–35

When Moses came down from Mount Sinai, with the two tables of the testimony in his hand as he came down from the mountain, Moses did not know that the skin of his face shone because he had been talking with God. And when Aaron and all the people of Israel saw Moses, behold, the skin of his face shone, and they were afraid to come near him. But Moses called to them; and Aaron and all the leaders of the congregation returned to him, and Moses talked with them. And afterward all the people of Israel came near, and he gave them in commandment all that the Lord had spoken with him in Mount Sinai. And when Moses had finished speaking with them, he put a veil on his face; but whenever Moses went in before the Lord to speak with [God], he took the veil off, until he came out; and when he came out, and told the people of Israel what he was commanded, the people of Israel saw the face of Moses, that the skin of Moses' face shone; and Moses would put the veil upon his face again, until he went in to speak with [God].

Commentary

Who initiates our inner encounters with God? Do we wait for God, or does God wait for us? For Moses, it is not an either-or situation; it is both-and. Sometimes Moses initiates the conversation and talks with God; at other times God initiates the conversation and talks with Moses.

The level of intimacy between God and Moses now reaches a point at which Moses belongs totally to God, and God has given the Divine Self to Moses in a covenant of friendship and love. The relationship is so intense that Moses is imbued, filled with God, even "contagious" or "drunk" with God. He is worthy to speak to others in God's name. Those who hear Moses hear God speaking.

Meeting a man or a woman of God can be an awesome experience, especially if one is suffering the effects of sin. The Scriptures say that the people are afraid to come near Moses. The people have repented for the sin of worshiping the golden calf. God has forgiven them abundantly, yet the blinding effects of sin are still evident. When the "appearance of the glory of the Lord was like a devouring fire on the top of the mountain," the people seemed to show no fear (Exod. 24:17). After their sin, fear haunts them. The piercing rays emanating from Moses' face both embarrass and frighten them. This is not an unusual phenomenon, as we know from these other biblical passages:

- *The Adam and Eve story:* After their sin, when they "heard the voice of the LORD God . . . [they] hid themselves from the presence of the LORD God . . ." (Gen. 3:8). Before Adam and Eve sinned, God's voice was joy to their ears; after their sin, it was a fearful sound: "I heard the sound of thee . . . and I was afraid . . ." (Gen. 3:10).

- *Joseph and his brothers:* When Joseph's brothers recognized him as their brother, whom they had sold, they were afraid: ". . . His brothers could not answer him, for they were dismayed at his presence" (Gen. 45:3).

Guilt caused by sin forces the sinner to withdraw, to lower the eyes, and to feel ashamed.

When Moses sees that the people are afraid to come near him, he calls to them, and Aaron and all the leaders of the congregation return to him. Afterward, all the people of Israel come near. Moses needs to again reassure the people of God's forgiveness. Only then are they ready to look at Moses and receive God's word.

A veil is mentioned three times in this scriptural passage. Moses removes the veil when he speaks with God and puts it back on when he is finished. He also takes it off when he speaks with the people and puts it back on when he is finished communicating God's word to them. The veil symbolizes marriage. It also symbolizes light and darkness. The light that radiates from Moses is infused by God and enlightens all those who have the eyes to see it. Yet that light is so strong that it can beam on the people for only short periods of time lest they be blinded. God takes care not to overwhelm the people.

The great symbol of God's light is the menorah, a seven-branched candelabrum. The details regarding its construction are significant. Two sets of three branches each reach out in opposite directions from a central stem. All the branches are turned toward the central stem, from which they receive their light.

Many meanings are attached to the menorah's casting its brilliance outward to a darkened world. God is the source of light from which all the other lamps receive their light. The first act of God described in the Scriptures is the creation of light: ". . . and the Spirit of God was moving over the face of the waters. And God said, 'Let there be light'; and there was light" (Gen. 1:2–3). The escape from Egypt is described in terms of light: "And the LORD went before them by day in a pillar of cloud to lead them along the way, and by night in a pillar of fire to give them light, that they might travel by day and by night" (Exod. 13:21). The great act of recreation enacted at Sinai is of light surrounding and emanating from God, casting its radiance onto Moses' face, onto the Israelites, and onto all the succeeding generations of humanity. The words that issue from God's mouth are clothed in light:

> Thy word is a lamp to my feet
> and a light to my path.
>
> (Ps. 119:105)

The menorah is also a symbol of the holy person whose face radiates divine light. Just as all the branches of the menorah are turned toward the middle stem, so the person who is turned toward God radiates divine light. The light is communicated through who the person is, through the words that issue forth through the person's mouth, and through good deeds the person performs. Truthful words and good deeds are beautiful to behold. Like lamps, they give light without losing any light of their own.

The unorganized, unruly crowd of Hebrew slaves who left Egypt have become a people of God, a kingdom of priests, and a holy nation. Although one people, not all of them possess the same gifts and talents. Not all of them attain the same intimacy with God as Moses does. It is likewise within the human personality. On one level we may be on the mountaintop with God, and on another level we may be immersed in the distractions of false gods and transient pleasure. Saint Teresa saw the human soul as seven interior castles. Hasidic literature describes five levels of the soul:

- *Nephesh:* vitality; the lowest grade and life force of the body. This is the natural soul.
- *Ruach:* spirit; the next level or the spiritual faculty, vivifying a person's emotional attributes.
- *Neshamah:* soul; the divine force, vivifying the intellect.
- *Chayah:* living; a more refined godly level.
- *Yechidah:* divine spark; the innermost point of the soul, which is united and one with God. It is the quintessential point of the soul. *Yechidah* is the divine spark itself burning in the most refined part of the soul. From this center, where God and the self meet, the light can come forth, enlightening all the levels of our self, drawing them into an integral wholeness, a oneness in the Lord.

Reflection and Journal-writing Exercises

1. Try to become conscious of all the life forces that power your being. Begin by getting in touch with the life forces that power your body.
- Concentrate on your breathing. Feel your lungs expand and contract as they reach out to bring in the air around you.
- Listen to and feel your heart. Feel it pulsing blood throughout all of your body.
- Feel any sensation in or on your body. Picture your brain sending and receiving the signals that trigger these sensations by way of a nervous system that extends from head to toe.
Next, get in touch with the energy that powers your emotions.
- Experience your present emotions. Name all of them that you can distinguish.
- Discern which emotion is strongest at this time.
Then attend to the power of your mind.
- Let thoughts and ideas cross your mind.
- Let some of them come to the front of your mind.
- Give words to some of your thoughts and ideas. Get them ready to be expressed.
Follow with attention to the powers that move your whole being, your motives, your desires, your aspirations.
- Name the primary forces that move you.

Finally, seek the center of yourself.
- Be as quiet as you can. Direct your consciousness inward.
- Imagine the wellspring of yourself, the still point within, the place where the new begins in you, the center where light meets light.

2. Imagine God, and the light of God, at the center of yourself. Pray to God each of the following:
- a prayer of thanksgiving
- a prayer of petition
- a prayer of contrition
- a prayer of praise

3. Write your prayers in your journal.

Memory Verse

Take this verse with you in your heart and on your lips:

Thy word is a lamp to my feet
  and a light to my path.

(Ps. 119:105)

TAV: *The letter* tav *is for* Torah, *or "Scripture"; for* tehilim, *"psalms"; and for* tephila, *"prayer." It is the last letter of the Hebrew alphabet and the last letter of the word* emeth, *or "truth." All God's words are truth.*

In the Beginning Is the End; in the End Is the Beginning

God gives the order to begin construction of the tabernacle. Moses calls the whole community together. The convocation is ordered, peaceful, harmonious, and eager. There is no account of warring or dispirited factions. Moses speaks to the entire Israelite community: cloth makers, water carriers, wood hewers, silversmiths, coppersmiths, carpenters, weavers, stonecutters, and every other kind of artisan.

They all gather. Such a flow of people coming from all directions! Everyone is busy, bringing and making, weaving and sewing, cutting and hammering. Previously they brought gifts for evil design in the erection of the calf, but now they bring them for good design in the erection of the tabernacle.

The transformation of the people that has taken place is remarkable. The picture of this gathering is in marked contrast not only to the making of the golden calf but also to the disintegration and suffering described in the opening scenes of Exodus. The people have made a long journey: from slaves to free people, from hate to love, from brother and sister against brother and sister to brother and sister with brother and sister.

The personal spiritual journey is similar. The beginning of the journey is marked by confrontation, by struggle between the multiple selves within: a slave, a Pharaoh, a Shiphrah and a Puah, an Amram and a Jochebed, a Miriam and an Aaron, a Dathan and an Abiram, and an immature Moses. As the journey progresses, so does integration: the shadow or evil inclination comes into harmony with the good inclination; the warring factions and conflicting ideas coalesce into an ever more peaceful synthesis. A wholeness, or "having it all together," is experienced. This is not to say that the wholeness will not come apart again in order to come together in another, higher synthesis. With each reintegration, there is a difference. The movement is from a fragmented, ego-centered personality to a wholesome, integrated individual; from naïveté and innocence to wisdom and experience; from isolation and loneliness to solidarity with God and all living creatures.

Throughout this meditation, ask God to show you the marvels wrought in your life through God's gracious love and mercy. Pray for the courage to continue the journey that has brought you this far.

Exodus 40:1–38

The LORD said to Moses, "On the first day of the first month you shall erect the tabernacle of the tent of meeting. . . ."

Thus did Moses; according to all that the LORD commanded him, so he did. And in the first month in the second year, on the first day of the month, the tabernacle was erected. Moses erected the tabernacle; he laid its bases, and set up its frames, and put in its poles, and raised up its pillars; and he spread the tent over the tabernacle, and put the covering of the tent over it, as the LORD commanded Moses. And he took the testimony and put it into the ark, and put the poles on the ark, and set the mercy seat above on the ark; and he brought the ark into the tabernacle, and set up

the veil of the screen, and screened the ark of the testimony; as the LORD had commanded Moses. . . .

Then the cloud covered the tent of meeting, and the
glory of the LORD filled the tabernacle. And Moses was not
able to enter the tent of meeting, because the cloud abode
upon it, and the glory of the LORD filled the tabernacle.
Throughout all their journeys, whenever the cloud was tak-
en up from over the tabernacle, the people of Israel would
go onward; but if the cloud was not taken up, then they did
not go onward till the day that it was taken up. For
throughout all their journeys the cloud of the LORD was
upon the tabernacle by day, and fire was in it by night, in
the sight of all the house of Israel.

Commentary

The completion of the tabernacle, a visible sign of God's presence, marks the time for the departure of the Israelites from
Sinai. God's glory fills this tabernacle, and the presence of
God—visible to all as a cloud by day and fire by night—leads
the Israelites forward.

The hallmark of this re-created people is their dependence
on the Spirit of God for guidance in their journeying. They have
reached a new and deeper level of spirituality where movement,
both physical and spiritual, depends upon dialogue with the Divine. This level of spirituality is operative in the lives of authentic people of God, women and men who live according to what
God wishes them to do in preference to their own desires. In
Saint John's Gospel we read, "'Truly, truly, I say to you, when
you were young, you girded yourself and walked where you
would; but when you are old, you will stretch out your hands,
and another will gird you and carry you . . .'" (21:18).

But will the people continue to journey in response to
God's Spirit? Yes, if they obey the final instructions given to
them at Mount Sinai, the most important of which pertains to

the Sabbath: "'Six days work shall be done, but on the seventh day you shall have a holy sabbath of solemn rest to the LORD . . .'" (Exod. 35:2).

The Sabbath safeguards the people from becoming absorbed in and enslaved to work. The command to keep holy the Sabbath day is given the first time in the context of imitating God. God does not become totally absorbed by the creative process, nor is God rendered completely passive by rest.

The Sabbath is also a proclamation of creaturehood. To stop work one day a week in obedience to God's command is to recognize that God, not the creature, is supreme. All does not depend on our own efforts.

The Sabbath is a sanctuary in time, a "great cathedral," a "holy of holies," a "shrine," which neither bombs nor fire can destroy. At the end of every six days the Sabbath continues to arrive.

The key to opening the door to the sanctuary of the Sabbath is contained in an abstention: you shall not do any work. To stop work is to be present to the "now," to be present to "what is." It is a form of contemplation—of being at one with self, with others, with the universe, with God.

The Sabbath can be further appreciated in terms of joy. We cannot make or force ourselves to be joyful. Joy is a gift to be received. All we can do is prepare ourselves to receive it. It is likewise with the Sabbath. We prepare ourselves to receive the Sabbath by a negative command: you shall not do any work on that day. The Sabbath is to be spent in charm, grace, peace, and great love. It is a day to reclaim our authentic state as a tabernacle of the Lord.

So, courage! A new journey from Sinai to the Promised Land is open before you. With God at your side and girded with sabbath observance and daily prayer, what is there to fear? In your end is your beginning—and what a beginning!

> We must be still and still moving
> Into another intensity
> For a further union, a deeper communion
> Through the dark cold and the empty desolation,
> The wave cry, the wind cry, the vast waters
> Of the petrel and the porpoise. In my end is my beginning.
> (Eliot, "East Coker," *Four Quartets*, p. 34)

Reflection and Journal-writing Exercises

1. Now that you have journeyed with the Israelites from Egypt to Sinai, skim through your journal.

- Highlight some of the most important insights you have received along the way.
- Mark the events in which God's presence was realized in your life journey.
- Describe transformations that have taken place in your thoughts and actions.

2. Reflect on how you have made a tabernacle of your heart, mind, and actions for God to dwell in and for God's presence to be manifest to other people.

3. Provide closure to this journey in prayer with a celebration (perhaps on the Sabbath, perhaps with the Eucharist) that both thanks God for the many blessings and mercies bestowed upon you in the journey just completed and anticipates those blessings in the journey still to come.

Memory Verse

Take this verse with you in your heart and on your lips:

Let me live, that I may praise thee. . . .

(Ps. 119:175)

Acknowledgments (*continued*)

Special thanks to the publishing team at Saint Mary's Press, whose guidance has brought this book to publication.

My final word of gratitude is to the students of the Faculty of Theology, University of Saint Michael's College, Toronto, who have contributed much to this work by their participation in "The Exodus Experience: A Journey in Prayer."

The scriptural quotations are from the Revised Standard Version Bible, copyright © 1946, 1952, 1971 by the Division of Christian Education of the National Council of the Churches of Christ in the USA, and are used by permission.

The excerpt on page 8 is from *Steppenwolf,* by Hermann Hesse (New York: Holt, Rinehart and Winston), pages 56, 57, 58, and 63. Copyright © 1963 by Holt, Rinehart and Winston.

The poem excerpts on pages 25 and 118 are from *100 Selected Poems,* by e. e. cummings (New York: Grove Press, a division of Wheatland Corp.), page 114. Copyright © 1954 by e. e. cummings. Used with permission from the reprint rights holders.

The extract on page 45 is from *Moses,* by Martin Buber (London: Horovitz Publishing, 1981), pages 58–59.

The extract on page 59 is quoted in *Studies in Shemot,* by Nehama Leibowitz (Jerusalem, Israel: Haomanim Press), page 143. Copyright © 1978 by the World Zionist Organization.

The poem excerpts on pages 82 and 149 are from "East Coker," in *Four Quartets,* by T. S. Eliot (London: Faber and Faber, 1970), pages 29 and 34, respectively. Used with permission.

The description of the five levels of the soul on page 144 is adapted from Hasidic literature, *On the Essence of Chassidus,* a free translation of an essay by Rabbi Menachem M. Schneerson (New York: Kehot Publication Society), page 23. Copyright © 1978 by Kehot Publication Society.